Making a Difference

HARCOURT BRACE SOCIAL STUDIES

Series Authors

Dr. Richard G. Boehm

Claudia Hoone

Dr. Thomas M. McGowan

Dr. Mabel C. McKinney-Browning

Dr. Ofelia B. Miramontes

Dr. Priscilla H. Porter

Series Consultants

Dr. Alma Flor Ada

Dr. Phillip Bacon

Dr. W. Dorsey Hammond

Dr. Asa Grant Hilliard, III

HARCOURT BRACE & COMPANY

Orlando Atlanta Austin Boston San Francisco Chicago Dallas

New York Toronto London

 Visit The Learning Site at http://www.hbschool.com

Series Authors

Dr. Richard G. Boehm
Professor and Jesse H. Jones Distinguished
  Chair in Geographic Education
Department of Geography and Planning
Southwest Texas State University
San Marcos, Texas

Claudia Hoone
Teacher
Ralph Waldo Emerson School #58
Indianapolis, Indiana

Dr. Thomas M. McGowan
Associate Professor
Division of Curriculum and Instruction
Arizona State University
Tempe, Arizona

Dr. Mabel C. McKinney-Browning
Director
Division for Public Education
American Bar Association
Chicago, Illinois

Dr. Ofelia B. Miramontes
Associate Professor of Education and
  Associate Vice Chancellor for Diversity
University of Colorado
Boulder, Colorado

Dr. Priscilla H. Porter
Co-Director
Center for History–Social Science
  Education
School of Education
California State University,
  Dominguez Hills
Carson, California

Series Consultants

Dr. Alma Flor Ada
Professor
School of Education
University of San Francisco
San Francisco, California

Dr. Phillip Bacon
Professor Emeritus of Geography and
  Anthropology
University of Houston
Houston, Texas

Dr. W. Dorsey Hammond
Professor of Education
Oakland University
Rochester, Michigan

Dr. Asa Grant Hilliard, III
Fuller E. Callaway Professor of Urban
  Education
Georgia State University
Atlanta, Georgia

Media, Literature, and Language Specialists

Dr. Joseph A. Braun, Jr.
Professor of Elementary Social Studies
Department of Curriculum and Instruction
Illinois State University
Normal, Illinois

Meredith McGowan
Youth Services Librarian
Tempe Public Library
Tempe, Arizona

Rebecca Valbuena
Language Development Specialist
Stanton Elementary School
Glendora, California

Grade-Level Consultants

Barbara Abbott
Adams Elementary School
San Diego, California

Janice Bell
Hammel Street Elementary School
Los Angeles, California

Carol Hamilton Cobb
Gateway School
Metropolitan Nashville Public Schools
Madison, Tennessee

Janet J. Eubank
Language Arts Curriculum Specialist
Wichita Public Schools
Wichita, Kansas

Billie M. Kapp
Teacher (Retired)
Coventry Grammar School
Coventry, Connecticut

Carol Siefkin
Garfield Elementary School
Carmichael, California

Grade-Level Reviewers

Esther Booth-Cross
School-Wide Coordinator
Bond Elementary School
Chicago, Illinois

Kristen Caplin
Murwood Elementary School
Walnut Creek, California

Nodjie Conner
Old Richmond Elementary School
Tobaccoville, North Carolina

Bob Davis
Office of Social Studies
Newark Public Schools
Newark, New Jersey

Maryfran Goetz
Notre Dame de Sion
Kansas City, Missouri

Patricia Guillory
Director, Social Studies
Fulton County Administrative Center
Atlanta, Georgia

Sharon Hamid
Williams Elementary School
San Jose, California

Nancy Kelly
Pinedale Elementary School
Pinedale, California

Mickey McConnell
Central Heights Elementary School
Blountsville, Tennessee

Gwen Mitsui
Solomon Elementary School
Wahiawa, Hawaii

Ronald R. Paul
Curriculum Director, Retired
Mehlville School District
St. Louis, Missouri

Ida Rebecca Ross
Woolmarket Elementary School
Biloxi, Mississippi

Marie Singh
Harden School
Salinas, California

Else Sinsigalli
Erikson Elementary School
San Jose, California

J. Mark Stewart
Social Studies Supervisor
Columbus Public Schools
Columbus, Ohio

Sheree Thomas
Cottage Elementary School
Sacramento, California

Renarta Tompkins
Morrow Elementary School
Morrow, Georgia

Contents

UNIT 1

We Belong to Many Groups 8

UNIT 2

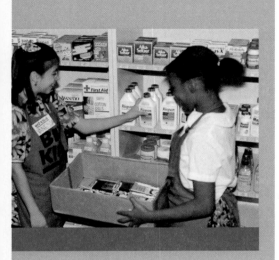

UNIT 5

Being a Good Citizen

UNIT 6

People in Time and Place

F.Y.I.

Literature and Primary Sources

Skills

Features

Maps

Charts, Graphs, Diagrams, Tables, and Time Lines

Atlas

Geo Georgie invites you to visit new places this year. The maps in this book will help you to know where you are. When you see Geo Georgie, stop and learn how to use the maps.

Come back to this Atlas often as you travel through your book. It will help you see where you are!

Atlas

The World

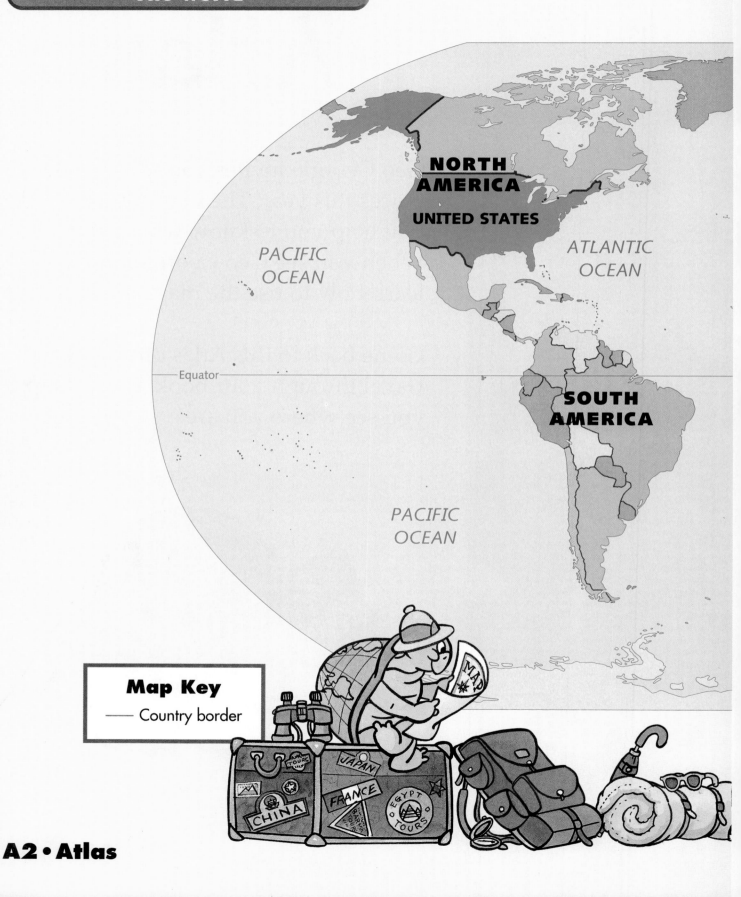

NORTH
AMERICA

UNITED STATES

PACIFIC
OCEAN

ATLANTIC
OCEAN

Equator

SOUTH
AMERICA

PACIFIC
OCEAN

Map Key

—— Country border

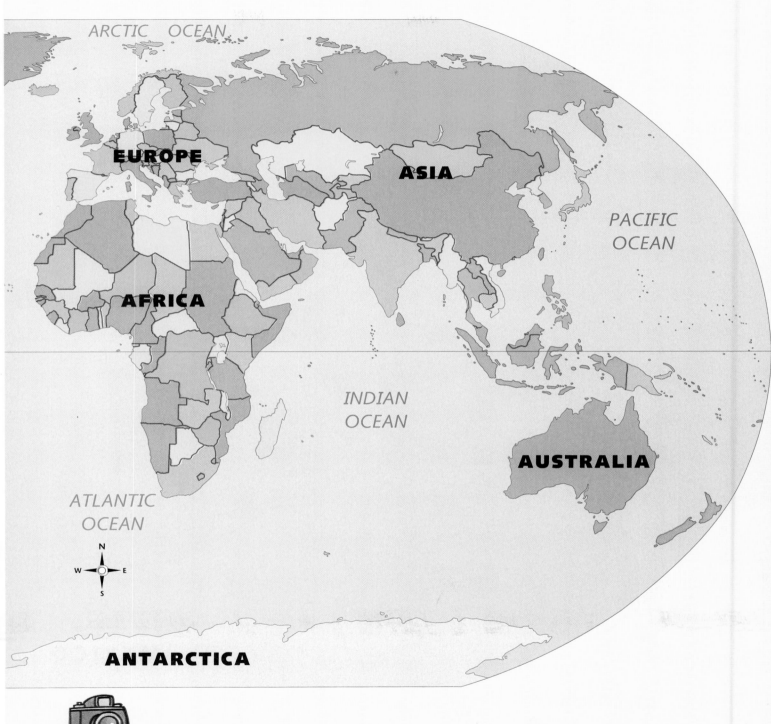

ARCTIC OCEAN

EUROPE

ASIA

PACIFIC OCEAN

AFRICA

INDIAN OCEAN

ATLANTIC OCEAN

N
W · E
S

AUSTRALIA

ANTARCTICA

Atlas

The United States

RUSSIA

ARCTIC OCEAN

Alaska
(AK)

CANADA

Bering
Sea

Juneau★

PACIFIC OCEAN

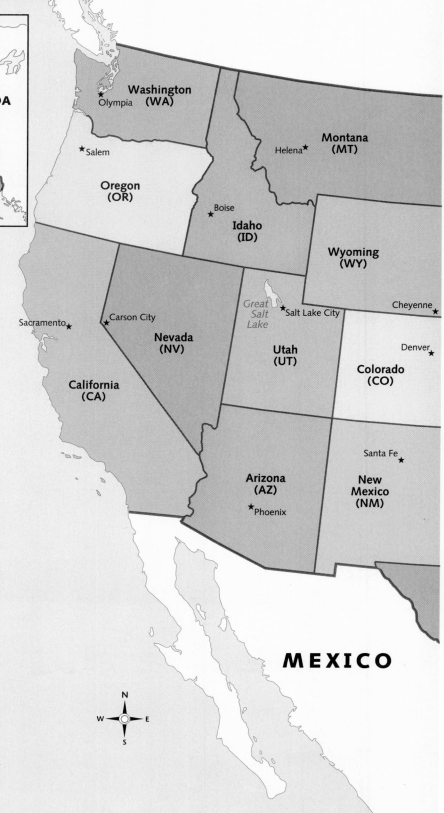

CANADA

Washington
(WA)
Olympia★

★Salem

Oregon
(OR)

Helena★

Montana
(MT)

Boise★

Idaho
(ID)

Wyoming
(WY)

Cheyenne★

Great
Salt
Lake

★Salt Lake City

Sacramento★

Carson City★

Nevada
(NV)

Utah
(UT)

Denver★

Colorado
(CO)

California
(CA)

Santa Fe★

Arizona
(AZ)

★Phoenix

New
Mexico
(NM)

PACIFIC
OCEAN

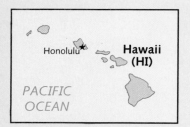

Honolulu★

Hawaii
(HI)

PACIFIC
OCEAN

MEXICO

N
W ★ E
S

CANADA

North Dakota (ND)
★ Bismarck

Minnesota (MN)
St. Paul ★

Lake Superior

Michigan

Wisconsin (WI)
Madison ★

(MI)
Lansing ★

Lake Huron

Lake Michigan

Lake Ontario

Lake Erie

South Dakota (SD)
Pierre ★

Iowa (IA)
★ Des Moines

Nebraska (NE)
Lincoln ★

Illinois (IL)
★ Springfield

Indiana (IN)
Indianapolis ★

Ohio (OH)
Columbus ★

Kansas (KS)
Topeka ★

Missouri (MO)
★ Jefferson City

Oklahoma (OK)
Oklahoma City ★

Arkansas (AR)
★ Little Rock

Kentucky (KY)
Frankfort ★

Tennessee (TN)
Nashville ★

Texas (TX)
Austin ★

Louisiana (LA)
Baton Rouge ★

Mississippi (MS)
★ Jackson

Alabama (AL)
Montgomery ★

Georgia (GA)
★ Atlanta

Maine (ME)
Augusta ★

Vermont (VT)
Montpelier ★

New Hampshire (NH)
★ Concord

New York (NY)
Albany ★

Massachusetts (MA)
Boston ★
Providence ★

Rhode Island (RI)

Hartford ★

Connecticut (CT)

Pennsylvania (PA)
Harrisburg ★

Trenton ★

New Jersey (NJ)

Dover ★

Delaware (DE)

West Virginia (WV)
Charleston ★

Annapolis ★
Washington, D.C. ⊛
Maryland (MD)

Virginia (VA)
Richmond ★

North Carolina (NC)
Raleigh ★

South Carolina (SC)
Columbia ★

Florida (FL)
Tallahassee ★

ATLANTIC OCEAN

BAHAMAS

Gulf of Mexico

CUBA

Atlas • A5

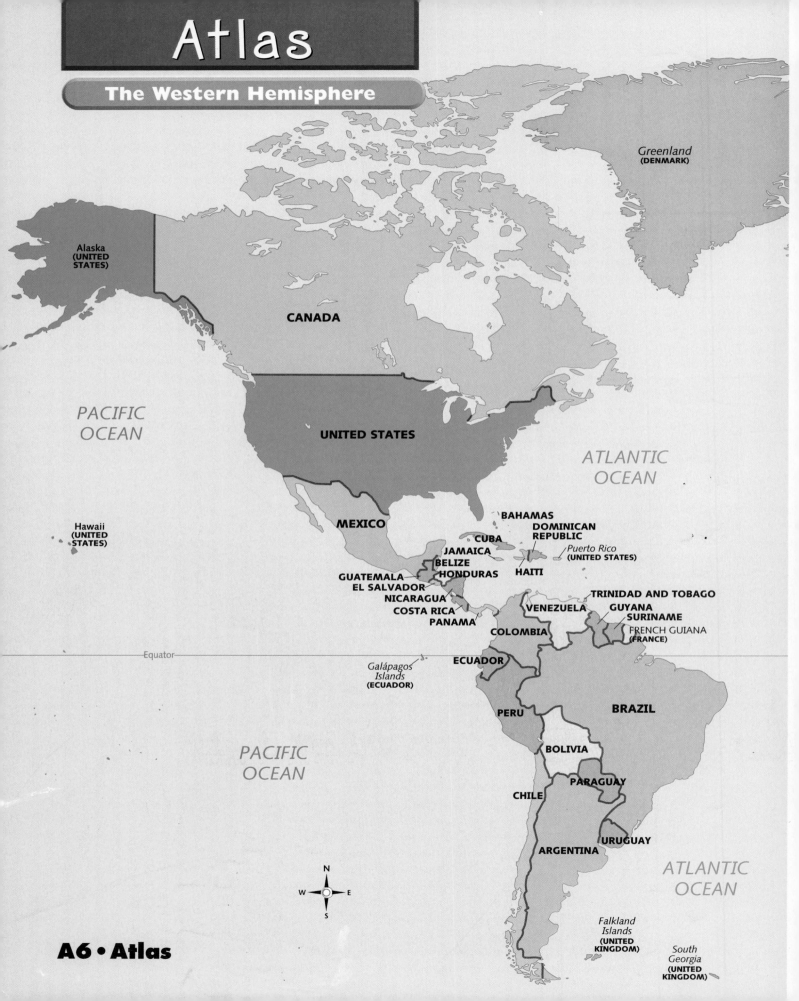

Atlas

The Western Hemisphere

Greenland
(DENMARK)

Alaska
(UNITED
STATES)

PACIFIC
OCEAN

CANADA

UNITED STATES

ATLANTIC
OCEAN

Hawaii
(UNITED
STATES)

MEXICO

BAHAMAS

DOMINICAN
REPUBLIC

CUBA

JAMAICA

Puerto Rico
(UNITED STATES)

BELIZE

GUATEMALA

HONDURAS

HAITI

EL SALVADOR

NICARAGUA

TRINIDAD AND TOBAGO

COSTA RICA

VENEZUELA

GUYANA

SURINAME

PANAMA

COLOMBIA

FRENCH GUIANA
(FRANCE)

Equator

ECUADOR

Galápagos
Islands
(ECUADOR)

PERU

BRAZIL

PACIFIC
OCEAN

BOLIVIA

PARAGUAY

CHILE

N

W   E

S

ARGENTINA

URUGUAY

ATLANTIC
OCEAN

Falkland
Islands
(UNITED
KINGDOM)

South
Georgia
(UNITED
KINGDOM)

Mountain

Forest

Lake

Valley

River

Plain

Hill

Desert

Ocean

Island

desert dry land with few plants

forest large area of land where many trees grow

hill land that rises above the land around it

island land that has water on all sides

lake body of water with land on all sides

mountain highest kind of land

ocean body of salt water that covers a large area

plain flat land

river large stream of water that flows across the land

valley low land between hills or mountains

We Belong to Many Groups

group
community
map
law
goods
services

group

A number of people doing an activity together.

community

A place where people live and the people who live there.

map

A drawing that shows where places are.

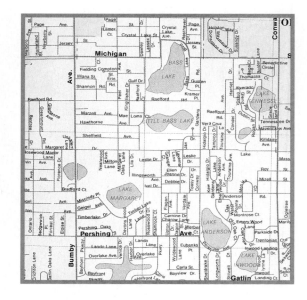

law

A rule that everyone must follow.

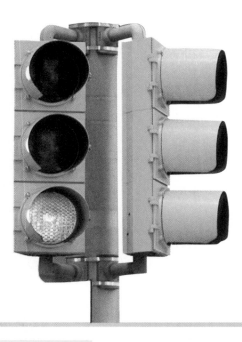

goods

Things that people make or grow.

services

Jobs people do that help others.

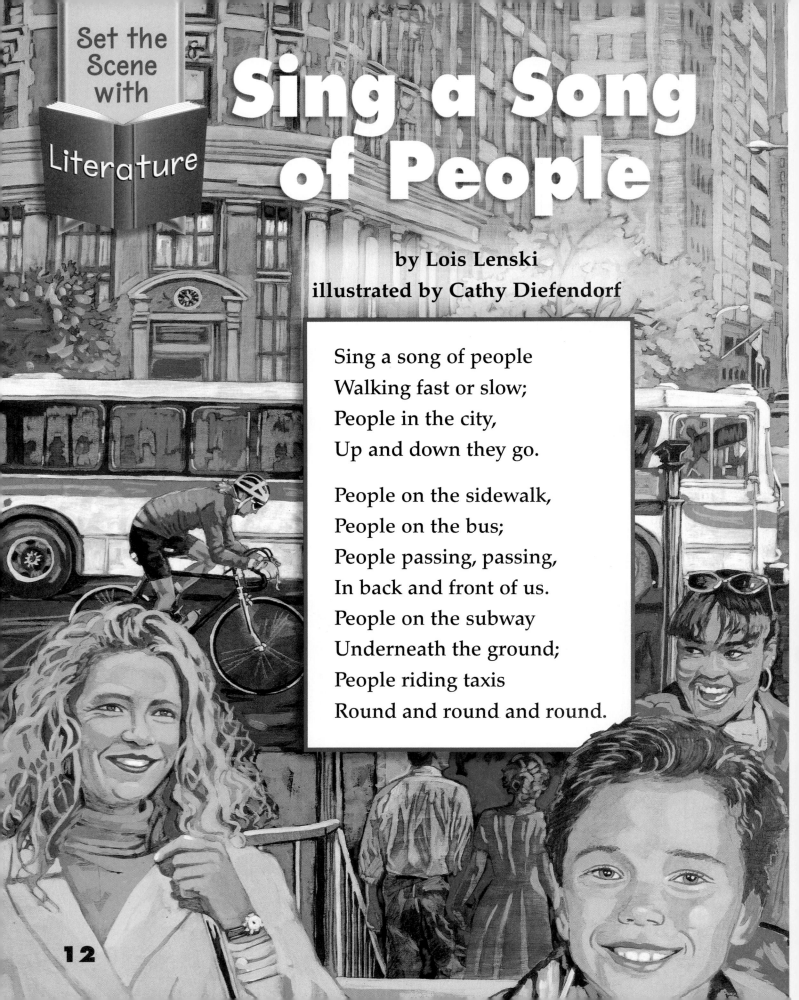

Sing a Song of People

by Lois Lenski
illustrated by Cathy Diefendorf

Sing a song of people
Walking fast or slow;
People in the city,
Up and down they go.

People on the sidewalk,
People on the bus;
People passing, passing,
In back and front of us.
People on the subway
Underneath the ground;
People riding taxis
Round and round and round.

People with their hats on,
Going in the doors;
People with umbrellas
When it rains and pours.
People in tall buildings
And in stores below;
Riding elevators
Up and down they go.

People walking singly,
People in a crowd;
People saying nothing,
People talking loud.
People laughing, smiling,
Grumpy people too;
People who just hurry
And never look at you!

Sing a song of people
Who like to come and go;
Sing of city people
You see but never know!

LESSON

1

Learning Together at School

2. title

3. story

1. lesson number

Visitors are coming to our classroom. We want to show what we can do. First, our teacher, Mrs. Warren, helps us make a plan. For some jobs we will work alone. For other jobs we will work together in a **group**.

4. new word

5. picture

We all make name cards for our desks. We get help from our art teacher.

Judy works on a calendar to show the activities of our busy class. She has marked our Open House on September 30.

September						
Sunday	Monday	Tuesday	Wednesday	Thursday	Friday	Saturday
			1	2	3	4
5	6	7 Spelling	8	9	10	11
12	13 Book Report	14	15 Guest Speaker	16	17	18
19	20	21	22	23	24	25
26	27	28	29	30 Open House		

6. main idea

My group is making a mural to hang on the wall. We want to show what we learn in school.

Everyone in my group has a special job to do. Juan is the leader. A **leader** makes sure the group follows the rules. **Rules** help us listen, share, and work together fairly.

7. detail

Biography

There are many ways to learn. Helen Keller could not see, hear, or speak until a teacher came to help her. Anne Sullivan made the letters of the alphabet in Helen's hand. Helen felt Anne's throat and learned to speak. Helen Keller wrote books and taught the world that all people can learn.

Juan is the leader.

Sandy and I make a list of the scenes we want to show on our mural. Then the rest of our group helps draw and paint the mural. Finally, we all clean the room and enjoy our work.

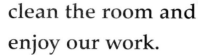

8. question

What Do You Know?

1. What does the leader of a group do?

2. How do you learn together in your classroom?

17

Living at Home and in the Neighborhood

You are part of other groups, such as your family and your neighborhood. A **neighborhood** is a place where people live. Lisa is making a model of her neighborhood. Read what she says about her home and neighbors.

My family works together to meet our **needs**. We need food and clothing and a safe place to live.

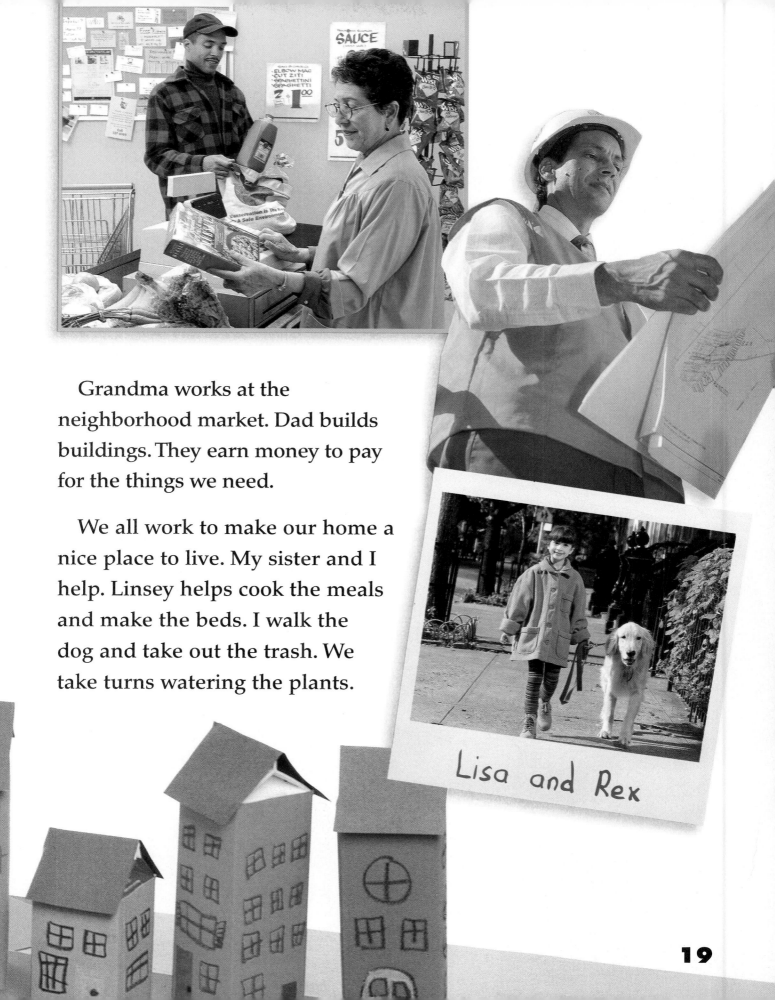

Grandma works at the neighborhood market. Dad builds buildings. They earn money to pay for the things we need.

We all work to make our home a nice place to live. My sister and I help. Linsey helps cook the meals and make the beds. I walk the dog and take out the trash. We take turns watering the plants.

Lisa and Rex

19

People in our neighborhood help each other, too. Our neighbor Ms. Lee gives me piano lessons. I feed her cat when she visits her daughter.

Our next-door neighbor is a firefighter. He helps save lives and homes in our neighborhood. Other people work as police officers to help keep our neighborhood safe.

20

Many places in the neighborhood help us meet our needs. We have a food store and a gas station. Sometimes we eat at the restaurant.

My neighborhood is part of a community. A **community** is a place where people live, work, play, and help each other.

What Do You Know?

1. What needs do families have?

2. How is your neighborhood like Lisa's neighborhood?

Learn from a Picture and a Map

We can learn about a neighborhood by looking at a picture.

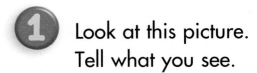 Look at this picture. Tell what you see.

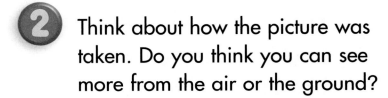 Think about how the picture was taken. Do you think you can see more from the air or the ground?

22

3 A **map** is a drawing that shows how a place looks from above. How are the picture and the map the same?

4 What things do you see in the picture that are not on the map?

Think and Do

Make a list of the places you see in the picture and on the map.

3 In and Around the City

Today Jesse went into the city with his mom. A **city** is a very large community with many neighborhoods. Read Jesse's journal to find out what he learned.

Morning

Time to go to the city. I fasten my safety belt.

Many cars, trucks, and buses are on the expressway. I wonder where they are all going.

24

I can't believe that so many people work in the city! Some work in small shops and stores. Others work in giant skyscrapers.

Traffic is moving very slowly. I see a police officer. Police officers make sure that people follow laws. Laws are rules for a community. I'm glad the officer is here.

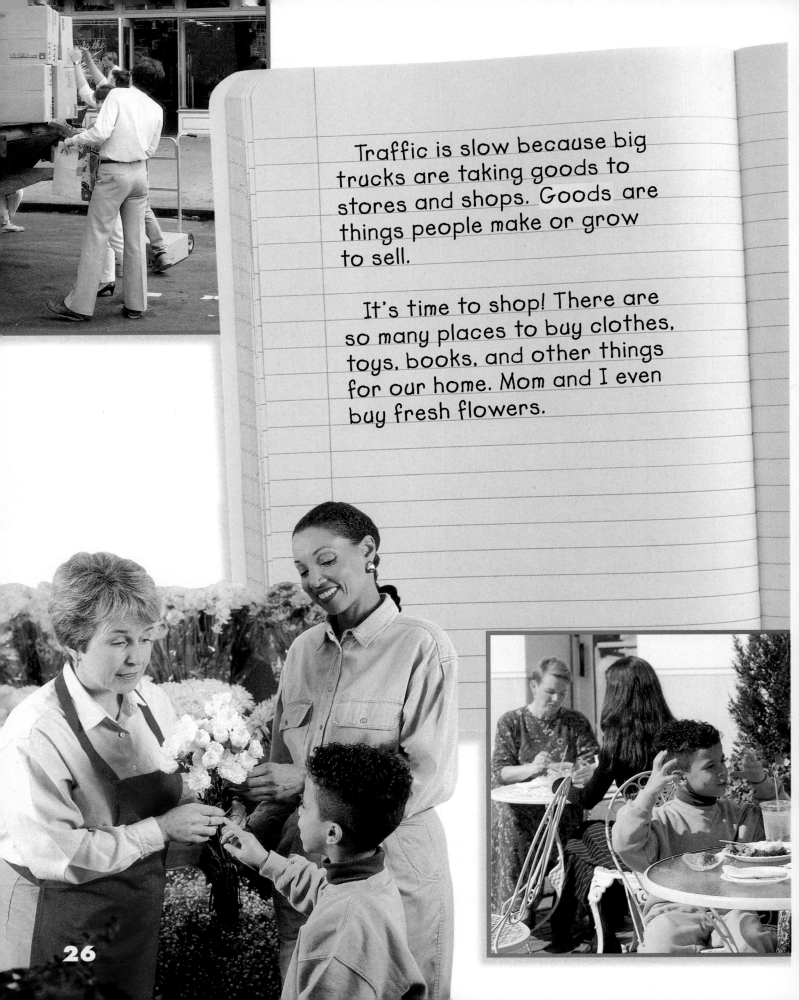

Traffic is slow because big trucks are taking goods to stores and shops. Goods are things people make or grow to sell.

It's time to shop! There are so many places to buy clothes, toys, books, and other things for our home. Mom and I even buy fresh flowers.

Afternoon

After lunch, Mom and I visit the Computer Museum. The guide tells us about a big computer map. A guide gives a service. Services are jobs that people do for others. I learned a lot from our guide.

Mom and I meet Aunt Leanne for dinner. We talk about the fun we had in the busy city. I can't wait until my next visit!

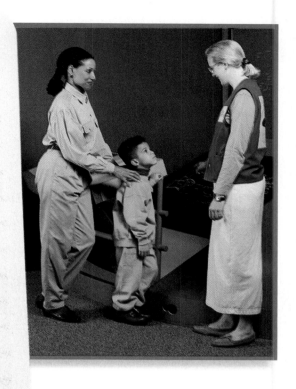

What Do You Know?

1. Name a service job someone might do in a city.

2. What would you enjoy doing in a city?

Read a Map

How do you think Jesse and his mom know where to go in the city? Perhaps they read a map. Maps help you find places. A **map key** shows you how to read a map.

1 What is the title of this map?

2 **Symbols** are pictures that stand for things on a map. What symbols are shown in this map key?

3 Find the symbol for the Computer Museum. On what street is the museum located?

4 Find the compass rose on the map. A **compass rose** gives the directions on a map. The four main **directions** are north, south, east, and west.

Map Key

🏛 **City Hall**

💻 **Computer Museum**

🐟 **New England Aquarium**

👪 **Pedestrian Mall**

🚌 **Peter Pan Bus Terminal**

🍴 **Pier 1 Restaurant**

🏛 **Quincy Market**

🌳 **Park**

▭ **Street**

5 In which direction would you walk to get from the Pedestrian Mall to Boston Common?

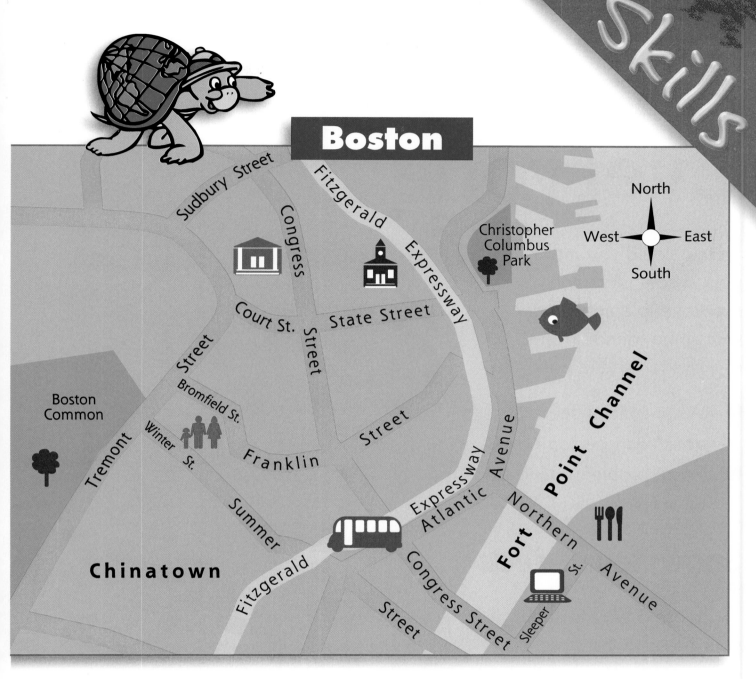

Boston

Think and Do

- Find City Hall. What streets would you take to get from City Hall to Christopher Columbus Park?

- In which direction would you go?

- What would you pass along the way?

A Park Is for Everyone

How could you make the park a safe place for everyone to enjoy? Work with some friends. Think of ways to use the park.

- What special needs does each person have?
- What problems need to be solved?

Show Your Ideas

Choose a way to show your ideas to the class.

- Make a model of the park.
- Write a story.
- Draw a picture.

4 Our Country of Many People

Our class made a collage of American citizens. **Citizens** are a group of people who belong to a community. We are citizens of our **country**, too. The United States of America has more than 250 million citizens.

Americans are different in many ways. We live in different places, eat different foods, and work at different jobs. But Americans are also alike in special ways. We follow our country's laws. We cooperate, or work together, to make our country a great place to live.

What Do You Know?

1. What is the name of our country?

2. How can you be a good member of this large group of Americans?

The Big Help

Megan Halbrook loves to help people. At school she looks for ways to help classmates. At home she helps her mom and dad with many jobs. Now Megan has some new ideas about helping others. She wrote about the ideas in a story for a contest at school. This is how Megan began.

"One day, when I was watching television, I saw something called The Big Help. I sat wondering what The Big Help was. Then they explained it. The Big Help was about kids doing community service. Community service is helping other people or helping the world."

United States

Woodinville, Washington

Certificate of Participation

This certifies that

Megan Halbrook

has earned honorable mention in the intermediate division of

Literature

Hollywood Hill Elementary PTA
Reflections Contest

given this 1st day of December 1997

Michelle Williams
Principal

Chris Selbeck and Jennifer Norton
Reflections Chairpersons

Megan saw children helping their community in different ways. They picked up trash, painted over graffiti, and helped people. Megan liked the last idea best. She pledged, or promised, to work five hours helping someone.

Megan's dad told her about a Day of Caring she could join in his workplace. On that day, Megan's father took her to the house of a seventy-five year old man named Ray. Ray could no longer keep up with his chores. Megan cleaned out drawers, vacuumed floors, and washed dishes. Megan said that helping Ray made her feel "very, very good inside."

What Can You Do?

 Find out how you and your classmates can help your community.

 Talk with your family about things you can do to help others.

Visit the Internet at http://www.hbschool.com for additional resources.

Picture Summary

Look at the pictures. They will help you remember what you learned.

Talk About the Main Ideas

1 People belong to many groups.

2 Children in school learn together in groups.

3 Families help each other in neighborhoods.

4 Cities are busy places where people live, work, and play.

5 Communities have laws for order and safety.

6 Our country is home to many different Americans.

Write a List Many people help you meet your needs. Make a list of some of these people. Tell how they help you.

Use Vocabulary

law
community
services
goods
group
map

Which word goes with each meaning?

1 a place where people live, work, and play

2 a drawing that shows where places are

3 a rule that everyone must follow

4 jobs that people do for others

5 a number of people doing something together

6 things that people make or grow to sell

Check Understanding

1 Name two groups to which you belong.

2 What people in the community help families meet their needs?

3 How do laws help people in a community?

4 In what ways are American citizens different from one another? How are they the same?

Think Critically

1 What might happen if there were no laws in a city?

2 Why should we respect people's differences?

Read a Map

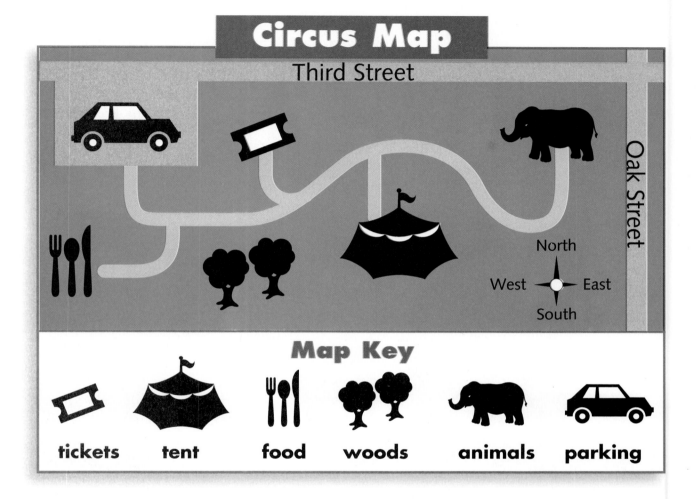

Circus Map

Third Street

Oak Street

North
West — East
South

Map Key

tickets   tent   food   woods   animals   parking

1. Does the map show the circus from the ground or from the air?

2. What symbol stands for a circus tent?

3. What is between the food place and the animals?

4. On which street is the parking lot?

5. What is east of the parking lot?

39

Apply Skills

Do It Yourself

Look at the picture. Make a list of the places you see.

Draw a map to show the places in the picture.

Make a map key for your map. Be sure to add a compass rose.

Share your map with a classmate.

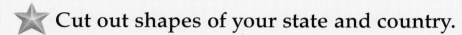

Unit Activity

Make a "World on a String" Mobile

Make a mobile of people and the groups they belong to.

⭐ Cut out shapes of your state and country.

⭐ Find and cut out pictures of all different kinds of people.

⭐ Glue your cutouts to pieces of yarn and tie them to a hanger.

⭐ Hang your mobile in the classroom.

Visit the Internet at http://www.hbschool.com for additional resources.

Read More About It

The Giant Jam Sandwich by John Vernon Lord. Houghton Mifflin. A tall tale shows how people in a community work together to solve a problem.

Marge's Diner by Gail Gibbons. HarperCollins. Interesting people come into Marge's diner.

Mrs. Katz and Tush by Patricia Polacco. Dell. A young boy helps a neighbor and learns that all people share the same feelings.

41

Where We Live

Vocabulary

geography
landform
continent
globe
resource
conservation

geography

The study of the Earth and its people.

landform

A kind of land.

continent

One of the largest bodies of land on the Earth.

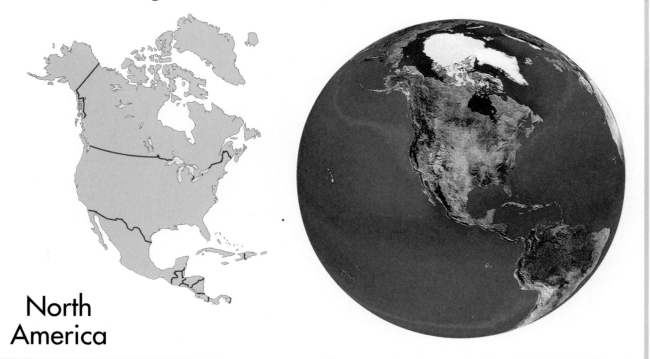

North America

globe

A model of the Earth.

resource

Something people use that comes from the Earth.

conservation

Working to save resources or make them last longer.

SAVE THE BEACH

Always Wondering

by Aileen Fisher

illustrated by Daphne McCormack

Roads run by
and paths run by
and tracks
where trains go thundering

Past green and brown
of field and town
and over-ing and under-ing.

Brooks run by
and creeks run by
and rivers
big and blundering,

And where they end,
around what bend,
I'm always, always wondering.

47

Looking Around Communities

The study of the Earth and its people is called **geography**. This photo album shows that people live in communities of different sizes.

A crowded city

Cities are big places with many people and lots of things to do. People live and work in tall buildings and travel on busy streets.

A suburb near a city

A **suburb** is a community near a city. It has quieter neighborhoods and less traffic than the city. Many people go to the city each day to work.

A small town

People also live in small towns or on farms. Neighbors in these places know each other. They help one another and have fun together.

Communities have different kinds of land near them. The land may be flat or hilly. The shapes of the land are called **landforms**.

Mountains are the highest kind of land. High places are colder than low places. The air at the tops of tall mountains is so cold that the snow never melts.

Tall, rocky mountains

Between mountains or hills are lower lands called **valleys**. People may live in the valleys.

A valley between mountains

50

A flat plain

Large, flat parts of the Earth are called **plains**. The land in most plains is good for farming and for raising animals.

Dry desert land

Deserts are dry lands that get little rain. They are often hot in the daytime and cool at night.

Communities may also be near different kinds of bodies of water. Water may be salty or fresh, flowing or still.

Oceans are the largest bodies of water. Their salty waves fall on beaches all over the world.

Ocean waves

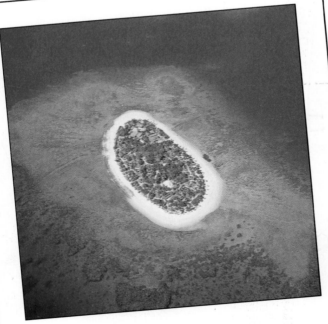

An island in the ocean

There are islands in some bodies of water. An **island** is a landform with water all around it.

A flowing river

Rivers have fresh water, not salt water. Rivers start as small streams. They flow down mountains and across the land to the oceans. Rivers can flow through towns and cities.

Sailboats on a lake

Lakes are bodies of still water with land all around them. Most have fresh water. Lakes can be many different sizes.

What Do YOU Know?

1. What is a suburb?
2. What pictures would be in a photo album of your community?

Find Land and Water on a Map

Maps often use colors and symbols to show different kinds of land and bodies of water.

ALASKA

1 Look at the map key. What color is used to show deserts?

2 Use the map key to find the symbol for mountains. Which side of the country has more mountains? Which ocean is it near?

PACIFIC OCEAN

3 Find some lakes and rivers on the map. Which body of water flows between the United States and Mexico? Which bodies of water are between Canada and the United States?

HAWAII

Land and Water in the United States

CANADA

ATLANTIC OCEAN

UNITED STATES

MEXICO

North
West — East
South

Map Key
⛰ Mountains
▢ Plains
▨ Deserts
▢ Lakes
〜 Rivers

Think and Do

Where are our country's longest rivers?
How do you think they help the land?

Life in Different Places

Three pen pals share what life is like in a mountain community, an island community, and a desert community. Read their letters.

Dear Felicia,

Hi. I'm glad you are my new pen pal. I live in New York. My house is in the woods. I took a picture of two raccoons in a tree in my backyard. Aren't they cute? It snows a lot in the mountains near my house. Does it snow in Grenada?

My mother works at an animal shelter. My grandfather works at the railroad in town. I like to swim and fish with my friends in the summer. In the winter we enjoy skiing. What do you do for fun?

Your pal,
Jared

Dear Jared,

   I live on a small island. I like to fish, too. My family has a fishing farm. On Saturdays I help my father and my uncle on our boat.

   Last week we had a big carnival in our town. Almost everybody came. Do you like my costume? My sister painted my face for the parade.

   I took a picture of some of my friends at school. It is warm here all the time. I've never even seen snow! What does it feel like? Please write soon.

                    Your friend,
                 Felicia

P.S. April is my other pen pal. She is writing you a letter, too.

Dear Jared,

I live with my grandparents in the Cochiti Pueblo in New Mexico. We live in an adobe house. It is very dry here.

Our class went on a field trip. We saw a place where people lived a long time ago. Their houses were built into the side of the mountain.

My grandparents make beautiful pottery. They sell it to people who come to see Cochiti Pueblo. I am learning to make pots and dolls out of clay.

Pueblo Feast Day is a special day. Everyone wears a costume. We all dance and sing. Maybe you and Felicia can come to a Feast Day. That would be fun! Please write.

Your pen pal,

April

What Do YOU Know?

1. How is the weather different for Jared and Felicia?

2. What would you write in a letter about where you live?

Use a Globe

The places you just read about are in North America. North America is a large land area called a **continent**. You can see continents and oceans on a globe. A **globe** is a model of the Earth.

Look at the picture of the globe. How does a globe look like the Earth? How is a globe different from a map?

2 Now look below at the drawings of a globe. How many continents do you see? Name them.

3 How many oceans do you see? Name them.

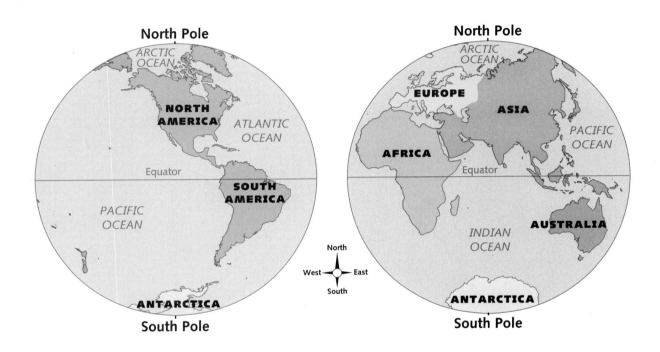

4 Find the North Pole and South Pole on each drawing. Then put your finger on the line drawn halfway between the two poles. This is the **equator**. It is a make-believe line that divides the Earth in half.

Think and Do

Find the equator on a globe. Which three continents does the equator cross?

3 Using the Land

The children in Jason's class brought pictures and other things from home to help them tell about their families. Jason told the story of how his family has used and changed the land on their farm.

Clearing the land

Plowing the field

Harvest time

A long time ago, our farm was covered with trees. My great-grandfather cut down the trees so he could farm the land. A company used the trees to make paper and wood products.

My great-grandfather worked on the farm every day. He worked from early in the morning until it was dark. First, he plowed the field to get it ready for planting. In the spring, he planted wheat seeds in the warm, soft soil. Farming was very hard work.

Rain and sunshine helped the wheat grow tall. In autumn, the **crop** was ready to be harvested. All the workers helped cut the wheat. Everyone celebrated at harvest time!

My family

Harvesting wheat on our farm

History

Long, long ago, farmers planted wheat in a dry land called Mesopotamia. They used plows pulled by oxen to make rows for the seeds. They dug ditches to carry water to the plants.

Farming is different for our family now. We have computers and new machines to help us. But farming is still hard work.

My mother has a job at the television station. She tells what the weather will be. It is very important for farmers to know when it is going to rain.

Our whole family works hard during planting and harvest times. Harvest time is the best time of the year!

I like to watch the machine pour the wheat into the trucks. The wheat is dried and stored in tall buildings called elevators. We sell the wheat to companies that use it to make flour, bread, and pasta.

I love living and working on the farm with my family. But my favorite part of farming is eating all the good foods we get from our land!

Loading the grain

What Do YOU Know?

1. How do farmers get the land ready for planting?

2. How do people use or change the land near you?

4 Where Does Our Food Come From?

Think about breakfast foods you like to eat. How many people do you think it takes to make that breakfast? Would you be surprised to learn that it takes hundreds?

Many people work to get food from the farm to your table. Some grow or make the food, some move the food, and some sell the food.

Follow the **flow chart**, which shows the path tomatoes take to reach you.

Vegetable farmers plant and care for the tomatoes.

Field workers use big machines to harvest the tomatoes.

Truck drivers take the tomatoes to a cannery.

Trains and trucks take tomato juice to markets around the country.

At the cannery, workers make the tomatoes into juice.

Foods come from all over the country and around the world. Fresh fruits and vegetables, meat, and milk products must be kept cold as they travel.

Foods may be changed before they are sent to stores. Workers freeze, can, or dry some foods.

After the food gets to the stores, more workers take care of it. Some make sure the food is still fresh. Others put the food where it belongs on the shelves. Other workers check out what you buy and take your money.

The last stop is your family's kitchen. As you enjoy your next meal, thank the many people who helped get it to you!

What Do You Know?

1. Where is tomato juice made?
2. What is your favorite breakfast food? Who helps get it to you?

How to Make an Apple Pie

and see the world

by Marjorie Priceman

The earth gives us many resources. **Resources** are things people use to make what they need. Find out how you can use the whole world as a supermarket!

Making a pie is really very easy. First, get all the ingredients at the market. Mix them well, bake, and serve. Unless, of course, the market is closed.

In that case, go home and pack a suitcase. Take your shopping list and some walking shoes. Then catch a steamship bound for Europe. Use the six days on board to brush up on your Italian.

If you time it right, you'll arrive in Italy at harvest time. Find a farm deep in the countryside. Gather some superb semolina wheat. An armful or two will do.

Then hop a train to France and locate a chicken.

French chickens lay elegant eggs—and you want only the finest ingredients for your pie. Coax the chicken to give you an egg. Better yet, bring the chicken with you. There's less chance of breaking the egg that way.

Get to Sri Lanka any way you can.

You can't miss it. Sri Lanka is a pear-shaped island in the Indian Ocean. The best cinnamon in the world is made there, from the bark of the native kurundu tree. So go directly to the rain forest. Find a kurundu tree and peel off some bark. If a leopard is napping beneath the tree, be very quiet.

Hitch a ride to England. Make the acquaintance of a cow. You'll know she's an English cow from her good manners and charming accent. Ask her if you can borrow a cup or two of milk. Even better, bring the whole cow with you for the freshest possible results.

Stow away on a banana boat headed home to Jamaica. On your way there, you can pick up some salt. Fill a jar with salty seawater.

When the boat docks in Jamaica, walk to the nearest sugar plantation. Introduce yourself to everyone. Tell them about the pie you're making. Then go into the fields and cut a few stalks of sugar cane.

Better fly home. You don't
want the ingredients to spoil.

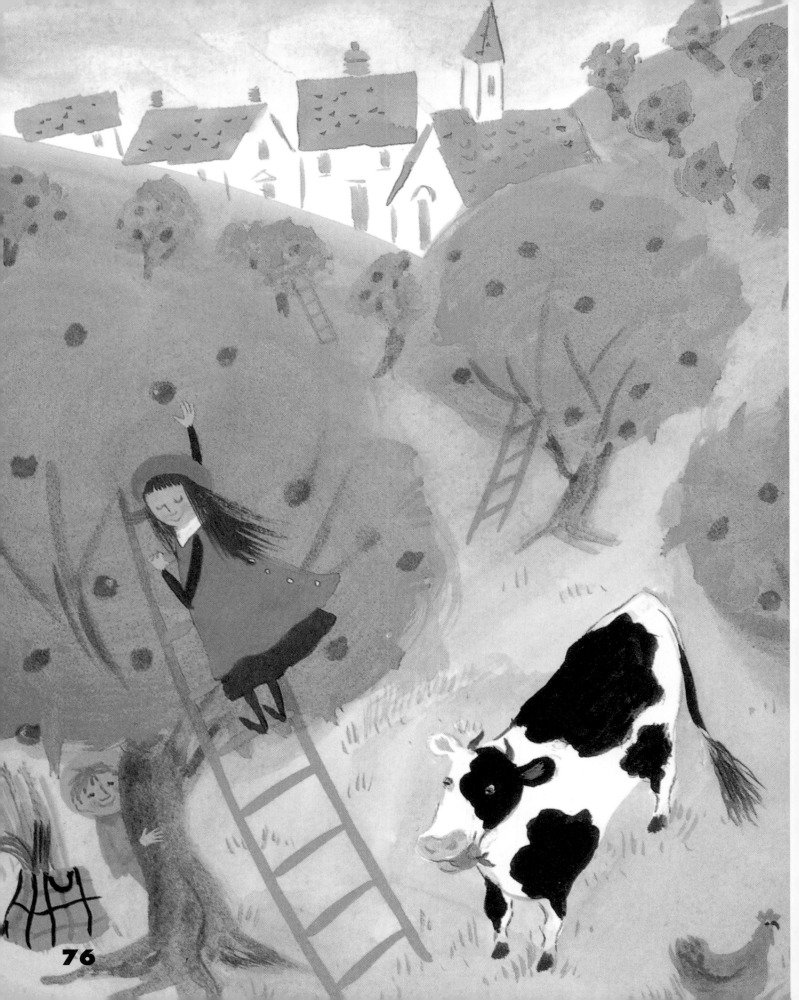

Wait a minute. Aren't you forgetting something? WHAT ABOUT THE APPLES? Have the pilot drop you off in Vermont.

You won't have to go far to find an apple orchard. Pick eight rosy apples from the top of the tree. Give one to the chicken, one to the cow, and eat one yourself. That leaves five for the pie. Then hurry home.

Now all you have to do is
mill the wheat into flour,

grind the kurundu
bark into cinnamon,

evaporate the seawater
from the salt,

boil the
sugar cane,

persuade the chicken
to lay an egg,

milk the cow,

churn the milk
into butter,

slice the apples,

mix the ingredients,
and bake the pie.

While the pie is cooling, invite some friends over to share it with you.

Remember that apple pie is delicious topped with vanilla ice cream, which you can get at the market. But if the market happens to be closed . . .

YOU CAN EAT IT PLAIN!

What Do You Know?

What resources were needed for the pie?

Read a Table

In <u>How to Make an Apple Pie and see the world</u>, you read about things we use from the Earth. You can use a kind of list called a **table** to find out about other important resources.

1 Read the title of the table. What does this table show?

2 What four resources are listed in the table?

3 Name two goods made from wheat.

4 What resource is needed to make plastic toys?

Think and Do

Some goods are listed more than once in the table. Which goods are made with more than one resource?

Goods Made from Resources

Resources	Goods			
trees	furniture	books	medicines	pencils
oil	fuel	plastic toys	pipes	medicines
wheat	flour	cereal	pasta	pet food
iron	paper clips	fire hydrant	pipes	tools

What Would Happen If . . .

Carlos Diaz's family owns an orange grove. They sell some of their oranges to stores. They sell the rest to companies that make orange juice.

In a group, talk about what would happen if there were a freeze. A freeze is very cold weather that spoils the oranges.

- What would the freeze do to the Diaz family?
- What would the freeze do to the store owners and the juice company?
- What would the freeze do to people who buy oranges and orange juice?

Show What Would Happen

- Write what each person would say about the frozen oranges.
- Write a newspaper story about the freeze.
- Draw before-and-after pictures to show what a freeze does to the trees and the oranges.

6 Caring for the Earth

My name is Nikko and I love trees. I have the largest collection of leaves in my second-grade class. Last week, I talked with a park ranger named Mia Monroe. We talked about conservation. **Conservation** is taking care of resources, such as the forest.

Nikko

Here are some things I found out about the job of a park ranger.

Nikko: Where do you work?

Ranger Monroe: I work in a national park. A national park is a place where the land and animals are protected. Visitors can see many kinds of plants and animals there.

Nikko: What do you like best about being a ranger?

Ranger Monroe: My favorite part of the job is telling children about the plants and wildlife in the forest.

Nikko: What else do you do?

Ranger Monroe: I look for people and animals that might need help. I collect water and soil samples to test. I also make sure that people follow the rules of the park.

Nikko: What are some of the rules of the park?

Ranger Monroe: People must not litter, pick flowers, or cut down trees. They must not tease or harm the animals. The rules protect the park so everyone can enjoy it.

Nikko: What tools do you use in your job?

Ranger Monroe: I use maps, a compass, and a two-way radio. I also use binoculars to help me watch the forest.

John Muir is called the father of our national parks. He taught people about the importance of protecting nature. He said, "Everybody needs beauty as well as bread, places to play in and pray in, where nature may heal and give strength to body and soul alike."

Ranger Monroe told me that some park rangers watch the forest for fires. In towers high above the trees, rangers look through binoculars for any sign of smoke.

It is important for visitors and park rangers to work together to keep the forest safe.

Fire tower

What Do You Know?

1. What is Mia Monroe's job?
2. What questions do you have about conservation?

Tree Musketeers

Can kids make a difference? You bet they can! My name is Sabrina. I live in El Segundo, California. My friend and I wanted to help keep the land and water clean. We started a group called Tree Musketeers when we were 8 years old.

United States

El Segundo, California

The Tree Musketeers decided to try to solve a big problem. El Segundo is next to Los Angeles Airport. There is a lot of noise and air **pollution** in our town from the airplanes flying over.

We learned that trees could help stop the pollution from coming into El Segundo. We planted a tree and named it Marcie the Marvelous Tree. We have planted more than 700 trees in El Segundo.

   **What Can You Do?**

⭐ Make a poster to show something you can do to help the Earth.

⭐ Read books about the Earth, such as <u>Michael Bird-Boy</u> by Tomie dePaola and <u>A Tree Is Nice</u> by Janice May Udry.

 Visit the Internet at http://www.hbschool.com for additional resources.

Picture Summary

Look at the pictures. They will help you remember what you learned.

Talk About the Main Ideas

1. Communities can be different sizes.

2. The Earth has many kinds of land and bodies of water.

3. People change the land.

4. People in towns and on farms depend on each other.

5. Important resources come from the Earth.

6. Conservation helps save resources.

Describe a Character Think of a character who might live in the picture. Tell where the person lives and works. Tell what the person does for fun.

Use Vocabulary

Choose two words from this list. Use the words in sentences that tell about the place where you live.

conservation
continent
geography
globe
landform
resource

Check Understanding

1 How is a suburb different from a city?

2 Name and tell about one landform and one body of water.

3 How do people change the land?

4 What workers help get food from farms to our homes?

5 Tell about something you use from the land.

Think Critically

1 How does geography help you learn about people?

2 How can you help take care of the Earth? Why is this important?

Read a Table

Trees		
Kind	**Size**	**Goods**
Maple	50–80 feet	syrup, furniture, boxes, musical instruments
Pecan	90–120 feet	nuts, floors, furniture, indoor walls
Pine	75–200 feet	lumber, turpentine, paint, soap, paper
Oak	40–90 feet	lumber, furniture, barrels, paper, railroad ties
Redwood	200–275 feet	outdoor walls, decks, picnic tables

1 How many kinds of trees are shown on the table?

2 Which tree grows the tallest?

3 Which tree gives us syrup?

Do It Yourself

Make a table. Choose a bird, a fish, an animal, or a flower. Use it as the title of your table. Write two facts about it in your table.

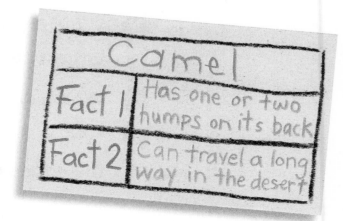

Camel	
Fact 1	Has one or two humps on its back
Fact 2	Can travel a long way in the desert

Apply Skills

• • • • • • • • • • • • •

Use a Globe

Look at the drawings of the globe and answer these questions.

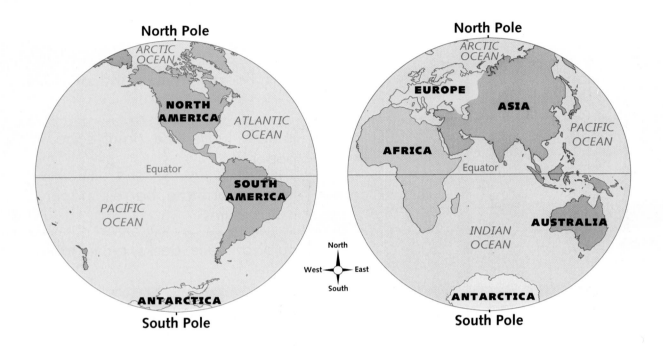

1. Is Europe north or south of the equator?

2. Which pole is in Antarctica?

3. Which two continents join to make up the largest land area?

4. Which ocean is south of Asia?

5. Which continents are completely south of the equator?

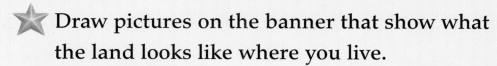

Unit Activity

Make a Banner

⭐ Draw pictures on the banner that show what the land looks like where you live.

⭐ Show how people have changed the land.

⭐ Find or draw pictures of things that grow on the land and goods made from them.

⭐ Hang up your banner and give it a title.

Mountain View

HARCOURT BRACE

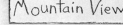

Visit the Internet at http://www.hbschool.com for additional resources.

Read More About It

<u>A New Coat for Anna</u> by Harriet Ziefert. Knopf. Anna's mother finds the resources needed to make Anna a winter coat.

<u>Johnny Appleseed</u> by Steven Kellogg. William Morrow. Legends tell about John Chapman, who planted apple trees for settlers long ago.

<u>Radio Man</u> by Arthur Dorros. HarperCollins. Diego goes with his family from farm to farm to help pick fruits and vegetables.

3

We All Work Together

Vocabulary

taxes
factory
transportation
producer
consumer
income

taxes

Money people pay to their government for services.

factory

A place where people make goods.

transportation

Any way of moving people or things from place to place.

producer

A person who makes or grows something.

consumer

A person who buys and uses goods and services.

income

The money people earn for the work they do.

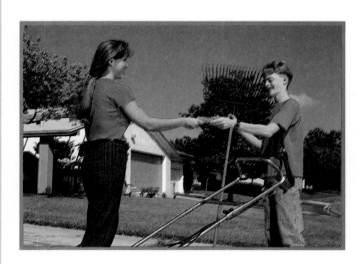

$ HELP $ WANTED

Responsible teen wanted. Job to include mowing and watering the lawn, weeding the garden, and some painting and light cleanup work. Please call 555-4321 to talk about wages and hours of work.

Set the Scene with Literature

Tea
Sarsaparilla
Calico
Brown Sugar
White Sugar

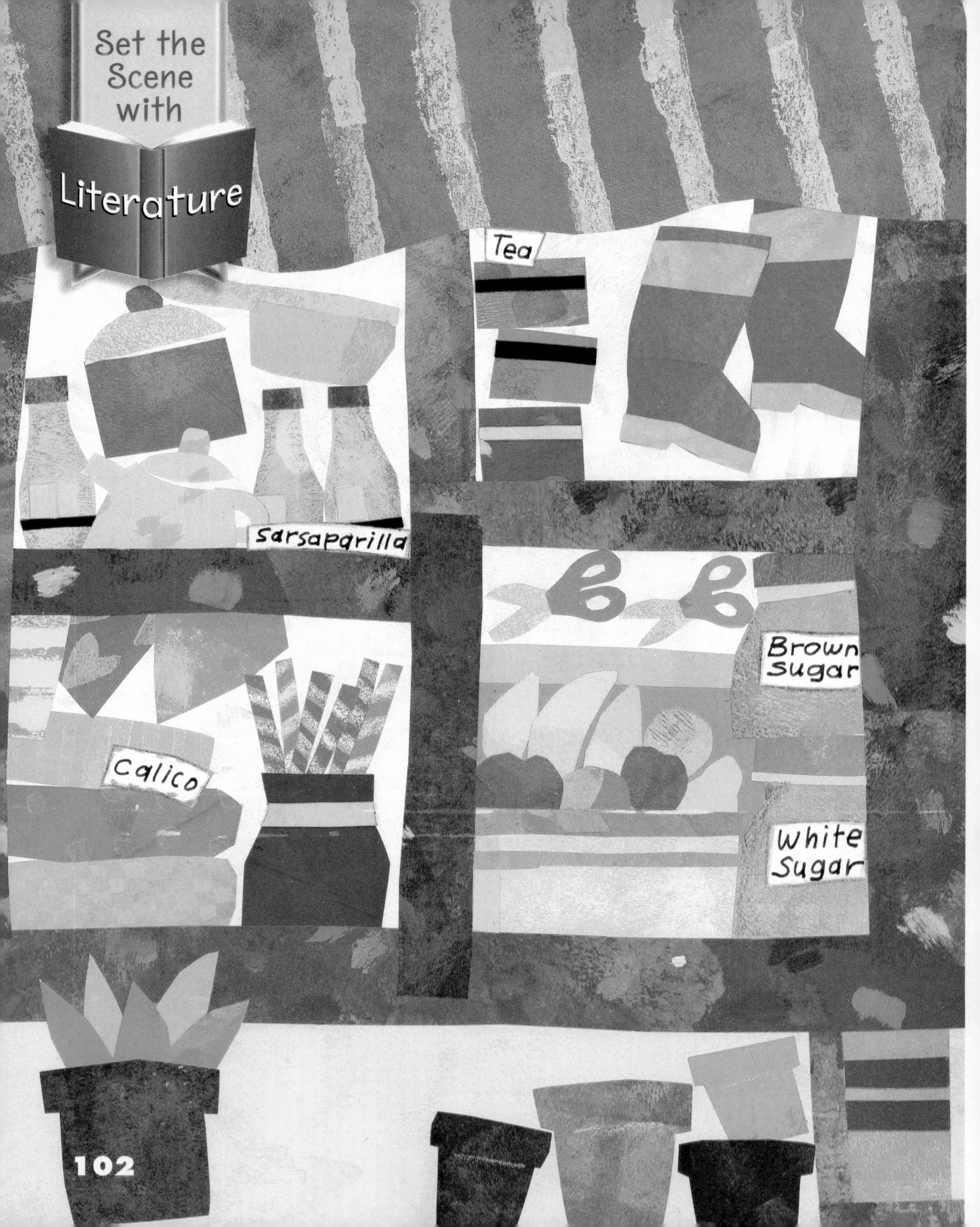

General Store

by Rachel Field

illustrated by Jane Conteh-Morgan

Some day I'm going to have a store
With a tinkly bell hung over the door,
With real glass cases and counters wide
And drawers all spilly with things inside.
There'll be a little of everything;
Bolts of calico; balls of string;
Jars of peppermint; tins of tea;
Pots and kettles and crockery;
Seeds in packets; scissors bright;
Kegs of sugar, brown and white;
Sarsaparilla for picnic lunches;
Bananas and rubber boots in bunches.
I'll fix the window and dust each shelf,
And take the money in all myself,
It will be my store and I will say:
"What can I do for you today?"

open

103

Community Services

My class has been learning about how a community pays for its services. We read this article in our weekly news magazine.

Taxes Pay for Community Services

Communities collect money from people who live there. This money is called **taxes**. Taxes are used to pay workers, such as teachers, police officers, and firefighters. Tax money pays our community leaders, too.

Taxes are also used to build schools and to buy police cars and fire trucks. Taxes pay for the care children get at health clinics. Tax money helps a community take care of its citizens.

"Tax money helps a community take care of its citizens."

What Do You Know?

1. Who pays taxes?

2. How do taxes help your community?

Use a Pictograph

Mr. Lee's class made a pictograph to show the places that give services in their community. A **pictograph** uses pictures to show numbers of things.

1 Look at the pictograph. How many kinds of services are shown?

2 Find the Key. What symbol is used to show the number of places that give each kind of service?

3 How many schools are there? Count the symbols to find out.

4 Are there more or fewer fire stations than schools?

Think and Do

Think of another kind of service you could add to the pictograph.

Services in Our Community

Bank	
Fire Station	
Hospital	
Post Office	
School	

Key

 = 1 service

LESSON 2

People Make Goods

Last week Josh's class went on a field trip. You can follow their tour to see how sneakers are made.

① A sneaker factory is a very busy place. A **factory** is a building in which goods are made. Each factory worker has a special job to do.

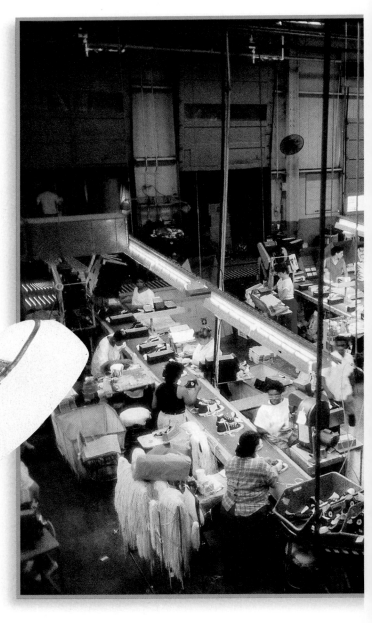

2 The factory buys rubber from countries that are far away. Workers pour melted rubber into molds to shape the sneaker bottoms.

3 Machines cut out the cloth top parts of the sneakers. Then workers sew the parts together.

4 Some workers punch holes in the tops for the laces. Others glue the tops and bottoms together.

5 More workers glue rubber strips around the sneakers.

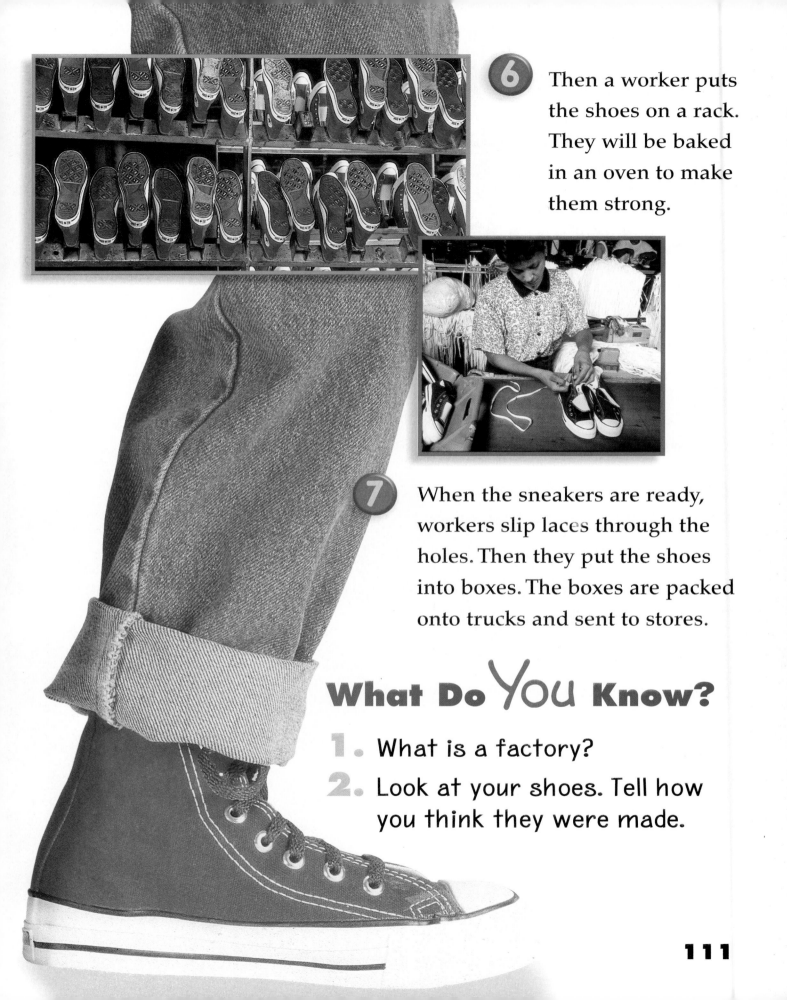

6 Then a worker puts the shoes on a rack. They will be baked in an oven to make them strong.

7 When the sneakers are ready, workers slip laces through the holes. Then they put the shoes into boxes. The boxes are packed onto trucks and sent to stores.

What Do You Know?

1. What is a factory?
2. Look at your shoes. Tell how you think they were made.

111

Predict a Likely Outcome

Kim got money from her aunt and uncle on her birthday. "Thank you," she said. "I'll use it to buy a new pair of shoes."

At the store, the shoe seller asked Kim, "What kind of shoes are you looking for?"

Kim said, "All my friends are wearing bright-colored sneakers. I want pink ones!"

"I am sorry," said the shoe seller. "We have only black sneakers and white sneakers. How would you like a nice pair of sandals?"

What do you think will happen next? What will Kim do? What will the shoe seller do?

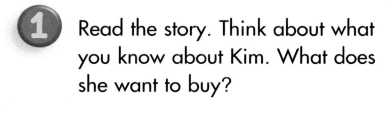

You are making a **prediction** when you say what you think will happen next. One way to make good predictions is to follow steps.

1 Read the story. Think about what you know about Kim. What does she want to buy?

2 Look for clues in the story. What does the shoe seller tell her?

3 Think about what will happen next. Make a prediction.

Think and Do

If a sneaker factory cannot get the rubber it needs to make its shoes, what will happen? Make a prediction.

113

Goods from Near and Far

Countries all over the world trade goods. To **trade** means to buy and sell things. The United States sells cotton, clothing, and food to countries such as China and Mexico. We buy cameras and machines from countries such as Japan and Germany.

Countries use many kinds of **transportation** to move goods. Goods travel by trains, planes, ships, and trucks.

My class has made a catalog of goods we buy from other countries. These goods come from all around the world.

Goods from Other Countries

Here is our class catalog. What are some goods we buy from Mexico, Scotland, and Japan?

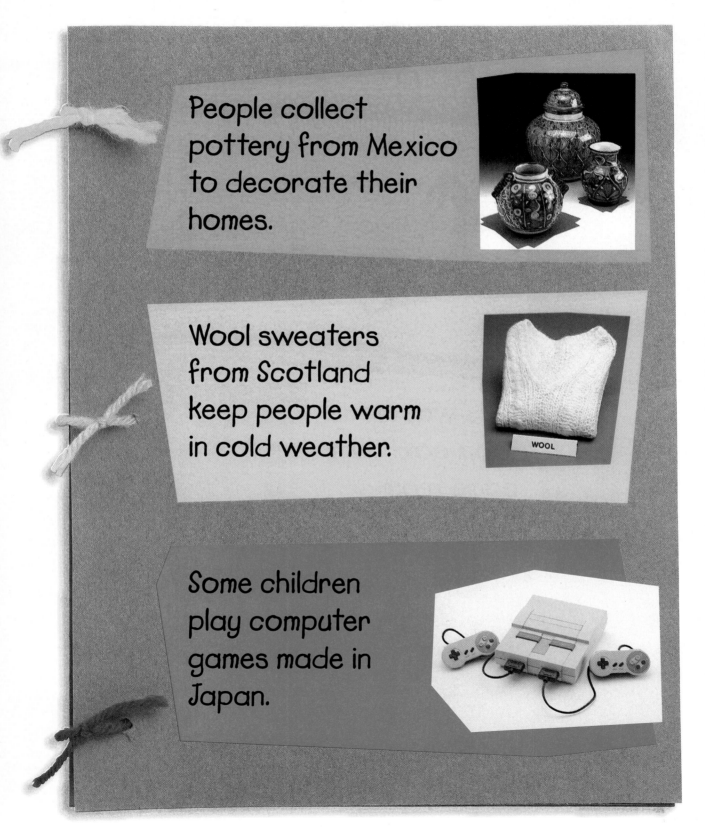

People collect pottery from Mexico to decorate their homes.

Wool sweaters from Scotland keep people warm in cold weather.

WOOL

Some children play computer games made in Japan.

Some countries have special foods, metals, or plants. Who might want tulips from the Netherlands?

These bananas grew on plants in Costa Rica.

This was made from gold that came from South Africa.

The Netherlands grows tulip bulbs to sell to other countries.

Sometimes we buy resources from other countries. American workers make goods from the resources. What might they make from these resources?

Chocolate is made from cocoa beans that grow in Ghana.

Rubber comes from trees in Malaysia.

A lot of our lumber is made from trees in Canada.

What Do You Know?

1. How do goods get from other places to the United States?

2. What goods from other countries can you find in your community?

Makers and Users, Buyers and Sellers

Our school raised money to help a sick classmate. Mandy needs a computer to learn at home. Everyone thought of ways to earn money.

Our class had an arts and crafts sale. We painted pictures and made clay pots to sell. I sold a picture of my dog, Red, for 25 cents. Our teacher said that we were producers. **Producers** make or grow things to sell.

We invited our families and friends to the sale. My sister bought two plants for her room. She was a consumer. **Consumers** buy and use things made by producers.

Today our school sent a new computer to Mandy. The money we earned helped buy it for her. The computer will make it easier for Mandy to learn at home.

25¢

$1.50

What Do You Know?

1. What do producers do?
2. When are you a consumer?

Kid Town

How would you plan a town?

Imagine that you and your classmates are building a new community.

- What goods would your town need?
- What services would it need?
- What kind of factory might help your town to grow?
- Which job would you choose?

Show your ideas.

Plan ways to show your new community.

- Draw a map or make a model of Kid Town.
- Wear special clothes or show tools for jobs in Kid Town.
- Act out consumers using goods and services in your community.
- Draw a picture of something your factory produces.

Kid Town Factory
Sunny Day Visor

Yarn Headband

Soft Beads

Cardboard Brim

Logo on Design

Making Wise Choices

Wants are goods and services that people would like to have. People cannot buy everything they want. They must make choices. Read to see how Jarrod plans to spend his money.

I earn money by washing cars for my neighbors. I also do extra chores at home, such as raking leaves. The money I earn is called **income**.

Jarrod's Car Wash

I spend some of my income. I keep the money in the bank until I want to spend it. Gran and Pops gave me money on my birthday. I am saving that money for college. I keep it in the bank, too.

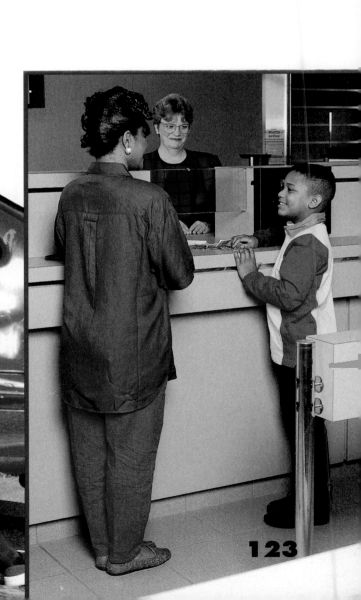

Jarrod's Bank Savings

Deposits

July 7
Money from Gran and Pops for college — $50.00

August 12
Money saved from allowances — $20.00

August 22
Money from lemonade stand and car wash — $35.00

When I shop, I see many things I want to buy. I make choices about how to spend my money. I do not have enough money yet to buy a new bike. And if I buy a fish tank, I will have to buy fish food every week.

I decide to buy a soccer ball. I like to play games with my friends. I will have money left over after I buy the ball. I take the money I think I will need out of the bank.

Mom and I look in different stores. There are many kinds of balls. Some cost more than others. I choose one that is on sale. It has been marked at a lower price to get us to spend our money in that store.

Four major highways and an airport bring many people to Bloomington, Minnesota. It is the home of the largest shopping mall in the United States. Nearly 12 thousand people work at the Mall of America.

Bloomington, Minnesota

United States

Baltimore, Maryland

Baltimore, Maryland, is on the Atlantic Ocean. Ships bring goods into its harbor. In 1896 the oldest shopping mall opened in Baltimore. Today people still shop at Roland Park Marketplace.

Now I think I made a good choice. I have fun playing soccer with my friends.

What Do You Know?

1. Where can you keep money that you save?

2. What do you choose to spend your money on?

125

Follow a Diagram

Have you ever wondered how money is made?
A **diagram** is a drawing that shows the parts of
something or how something is made. This diagram
shows the parts of a coin.

reeded ridge

face

U.S. motto

mint date

mint mark

Latin motto
("Out of many,
one")

eagle

Look at a penny, a nickel, and
a dime. How are they like the
quarter? How are they different?

This diagram
shows how coins
are minted, or made.

1 A carving machine carves the design of each side onto a steel stamp.

2 A cutting machine cuts bars of metal into blank coins.

3 A stamping machine stamps the designs on both sides of the blank coins.

4 A counting machine counts the coins into bags to go to the bank.

Think and Do

Design your own coin or paper money. Draw a diagram to show the different parts.

127

Biz Kid$

One store in Orlando, Florida, is completely run by children. It's called BIZ KID$. Everyone from the greeter to the check-out person is in the fifth grade.

United States

Orlando, Florida

Working at BIZ KID$ is part of a social studies class. The fifth graders are taught how to run a business. A **business** is a place that sells goods or services. At BIZ KID$ students learn how to greet people, count money, sell goods to customers, use a cash register, and get along with other workers.

Students say that working at BIZ KID$ is fun, and they learn a lot about business, too. Some of the goods fifth graders sell are snacks, first-aid supplies, and Earth-friendly products. At the end of the year, the students decide how they will spend the money they made.

What Can You Do?

⭐ Write to find out more about BIZ KID$.

⭐ Start a class business, and vote on what to do with the money you make.

 Visit the Internet at http://www.hbschool.com for additional resources.

Picture Summary

Look at the pictures. They will help you remember what you learned.

Talk About the Main Ideas

1 Service workers keep people in communities healthy and safe.

2 Workers in factories make many things people need.

3 People trade goods and money for what they want.

4 Producers and consumers need each other.

5 People make choices about how to spend their money.

Think and Draw Think of a job you might want to do someday. Draw a picture that shows the machines or tools you would use.

Use Vocabulary

Which word goes with each box?

consumer   **factory**   **transportation**
producer   **income**   **taxes**

1 train, ship, truck, airplane

2 money someone earns

3 building in which things are made

4 farmer, baker, quilt maker

5 buyer and user of products

6 money people pay to a community

Check Understanding

1 How do taxes help a community?

2 Why are factories important to people?

3 Why do countries trade goods?

4 Name a product that comes from another country. Tell how it might get here.

5 Why must consumers make choices about spending money?

Think Critically

1 Tell how a producer can also be a consumer.

2 Predict what would happen if people did not pay taxes.

Use a Pictograph

Services in Johnson City

Library	🏢 🏢 🏢
Fire Station	🏢 🏢 🏢 🏢
Police Station	🏢 🏢 🏢
School	🏢 🏢 🏢 🏢 🏢
Hospital	🏢 🏢

Key

🏢 = 1 service

1 What kinds of services does Johnson City provide?

2 How many libraries are there?

3 Are there more fire stations or police stations? How many more?

Do It Yourself

Find out how many libraries, schools, hospitals, fire stations, and police stations are in your community. Make a pictograph to show what you found out.

133

Apply Skills

Read a Diagram

1 Whose picture is on the five-dollar bill?

2 How many times is the amount written on one side of the bill?

3 What is the number of the bank that gave out the money?

4 What is the serial number of this bill?

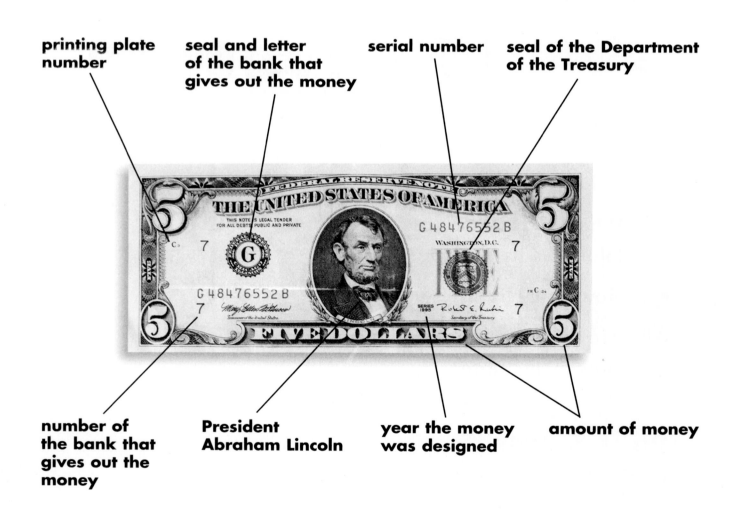

printing plate number

seal and letter of the bank that gives out the money

serial number

seal of the Department of the Treasury

number of the bank that gives out the money

President Abraham Lincoln

year the money was designed

amount of money

·········· Unit Activity ··········

Make a Career Day Collage

⭐ Find or draw pictures of workers who make goods and workers who give services.

⭐ Find or draw pictures of the tools workers use or special clothes they wear in their jobs.

⭐ Cut out and paste your pictures to large pieces of construction paper or poster board.

⭐ Hang the collages and talk about workers who make goods. Talk about workers who give services.

HARCOURT BRACE

Visit the Internet at
http://www.hbschool.com
for additional resources.

Read More About It

<u>We Keep a Store</u> by Anne Shelby. Orchard. Everyone in a family works together to run a country store.

<u>Market!</u> by Ted Lewin. Lothrop, Lee & Shepard. All around the world, markets sell different kinds of goods.

<u>Music, Music for Everyone</u> by Vera B. Williams. Greenwillow. Rosa and her friends start a band that plays at parties. Best of all, they get paid!

135

People Make History

Vocabulary

history
settler
landmark
President
invention

history

The story of what has happened in a place.

settler

A person who makes a home in a new place.

landmark

A familiar object at a place.

President

The leader of the United States.

invention

Something that has been made for the first time.

140

I Can

by Mari Evans
illustrated by
Melodye Rosales

I can
be anything
I can
do anything
I can
think
anything
big
or tall
OR
high or low
WIDE
or narrow
fast or slow
because I
CAN
and
I
WANT
TO!

141

American Indians

History is made up of the stories people tell about the past. Some stories happened long ago. Others took place even farther back in time.

The history of the American Indians starts long before the United States was a country. We call these people Native Americans because they were the first people to live in what is now America.

Today there are many different groups of American Indians. Each group has its own history and its own way of living. There were many groups of American Indians long ago, too. The table on page 143 shows some groups and the different clothing they wore, foods they ate, and shelters they built. A **shelter** is a place where people live.

Indian Group				
Powhatan	**Creek**	**Navajo**	**Chumash**	**Chinook**

Foods

Shelters

Clothing

143

"The First Thanksgiving" by Jennie Brownscombe

When the Pilgrims moved from Europe to America, they found the Wampanoag Indians already living here. The Wampanoags became the Pilgrims' friends. They taught the Pilgrims how to hunt and fish and to plant crops. The Wampanoags ate mostly corn. They wore clothes made of animal skins and lived in wigwams made of tree bark.

Biography

An Indian named Tisquantum, or Squanto for short, helped the Pilgrims and the Wampanoags become friends. Without his help, the Pilgrims might not have lived through their first winter. He taught them the Indian ways of living. Squanto and other Indians joined the Pilgrims for a thanksgiving dinner to celebrate the Pilgrims' first harvest.

144

People learn history in different ways. Some read stories written in books. Many American Indians learn their history from stories told aloud. They learn about the past through stories passed from grandparents to parents to children.

What Do **You** Know?

1. What Indian group helped the Pilgrims?

2. How can telling stories help people learn history?

Read a Time Line

A **time line** shows the order in which things happened. This time line tells the story of the Pilgrims.

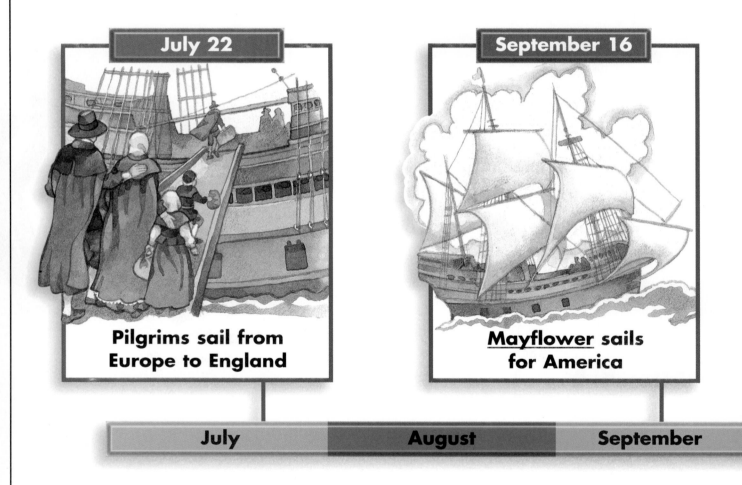

July 22

Pilgrims sail from Europe to England

September 16

Mayflower sails for America

| July | August | September |

1 How much time is shown on the time line?

2 In what month did the <u>Mayflower</u> leave for America?

3 In November the Pilgrims signed a plan for ruling the new settlement. What was it called?

November 21

Mayflower Compact is signed

December 25

Pilgrims land at Plymouth

October	November	December

Think and Do

How many months were the Pilgrims sailing on the <u>Mayflower</u>?

2 We Remember the Past

As time passed, American Indians saw new communities grow up in America. Compare daily life in one early community with the way you live.

Many years ago people came from other countries to live in America. These early American **settlers** built their own houses and grew their own food. They burned wood to cook food and heat their homes. Families dried, smoked, and salted some foods to store them for the winter. How does your family store food?

growing food

storing food for the winter

Getting clothing was a lot more work back then! Early Americans sheared sheep for wool. They spun the wool into thread. Then they wove the thread into cloth on a loom and made the cloth into clothing. How does your family get the clothes you need?

shearing sheep for wool

spinning wool into thread

weaving cloth

Most towns printed a newspaper.
The newspaper was one way people
learned about their community
and the world. How do people
get news today?

Early American settlers enjoyed some of the same things we do. They played games with their friends. Families spent time together.

What Do You Know?

1. How did early settlers get food ready to store for winter?

2. Could the early American settlers do what you like to do? Why or why not?

Read a History Map

Maps can show where places of long ago were. The first English settlers in North America built their colonies along the Atlantic Ocean. A **colony** is a place ruled by another country.

1 What year does this map show?

2 How many English colonies were there?

3 In which colony was Jamestown?
In which colony was Plymouth?

4 Which colony was the farthest south?

Think and Do

- Write these cities on a sheet of paper— Baltimore, Boston, Charles Town, Philadelphia, Williamsburg.

- Find out in which colony each city began. Write the name of the colony next to the city.

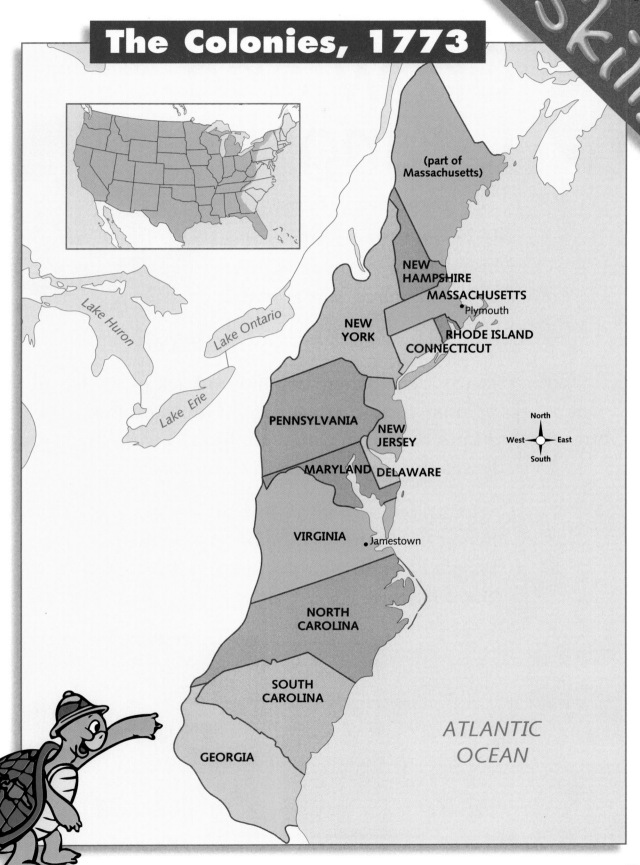

The Colonies, 1773

(part of Massachusetts)

NEW HAMPSHIRE

MASSACHUSETTS
• Plymouth

NEW YORK

RHODE ISLAND
CONNECTICUT

Lake Huron

Lake Ontario

Lake Erie

PENNSYLVANIA

NEW JERSEY

MARYLAND   DELAWARE

VIRGINIA   • Jamestown

NORTH CAROLINA

SOUTH CAROLINA

GEORGIA

ATLANTIC OCEAN

North
West — East
South

Communities Grow and Change

San Diego is a very old city in California. Join Miguel as he learns how the city has changed and grown.

Miguel: How old is our city, Grandpa?

Grandpa: San Diego began way back in 1769 as a Spanish fort. A priest named Junípero Serra built a kind of church called a mission inside the fort. It was the first mission in California.

Later, Spanish and Mexican settlers came to live at the bottom of the hill below the fort. People can still visit that area. It is called Old Town Historic Park.

San Diego Mission

Old Town

Miguel: Walking through Old Town is fun. I like to walk down by the water, too. I can see many kinds of boats sailing in and out of the harbor.

Grandpa: San Diego Bay has been important to our city. In the beginning, trade ships carried goods to and from California. Later, tuna fishing brought canning factories to San Diego. Now, many people have jobs at the Naval Base.

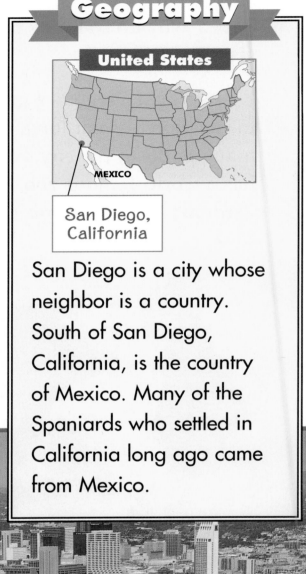

Geography

United States

San Diego, California

San Diego is a city whose neighbor is a country. South of San Diego, California, is the country of Mexico. Many of the Spaniards who settled in California long ago came from Mexico.

Miguel: Why do so many people visit San Diego?

Grandpa: San Diego is a good place to vacation all year long. There are many parks in the city. Balboa Park has a world-famous zoo, colorful gardens, and museums.

Convention Center

Also, the people of San Diego built a large Convention Center. Groups travel from all over the country to meetings there. Everyone likes to come to a city that has interesting places to visit, good weather, and beautiful beaches.

Mexican Museum mural art

Old Point Loma Lighthouse

Miguel: What is your favorite place, Grandpa?

Grandpa: My favorite landmark is the Old Point Loma Lighthouse. A **landmark** is something people easily see and know as part of the community. The lighthouse is near the Cabrillo National Monument by San Diego Bay. Both landmarks remind us of Juan Rodríguez Cabrillo, who sailed into the bay in 1542. That was more than 200 years before the first mission was built.

Miguel: I like to look out from Point Loma and see our beautiful city. Think how much it has changed!

What Do YOU Know?

1. From what country were the people who built the first fort and mission in San Diego?

2. What are some landmarks in your community?

Find Cause and Effect

Changes happen for different reasons. What makes something happen is a **cause**. What happens is an **effect**.

 1 Look at the first picture. This is how San Diego looked long ago. What was the community like?

2 Why do you think a railroad was built to San Diego?

3 The picture below shows San Diego a few years later. What caused the community to grow?

Think and Do

What changes do you think you would see in San Diego today? Why?

San Diego from Cor. of 6th and Ash Sts.

4

People Lead the Way

Washington, D.C., is our nation's capital. A **capital** is a city where the leaders of a country work. Come along as we tour this special city in our country's history.

Here is the White House, where the President lives. The **President** is the leader of the United States. Many Presidents have lived in the White House since it was built in 1800. The building has been changed many times. Our country has changed, too.

The White House

The Capitol Building

This is the Capitol Building where the lawmakers work. **Lawmakers** are people who make the laws of our country. The Capitol Building has had three different domes. The dome is a symbol of our great country.

Congress

The **Congress** is the group of lawmakers who work in the Capitol Building. They are some of the leaders who help our country grow and change. They plan ways to keep our country strong.

This part of the city is called the West Mall. It is not a mall for shopping. People come here to see the monuments. **Monuments** are places or buildings built to honor someone. The Washington Monument and the Lincoln and Jefferson memorials honor three great Presidents. Each one helped lead our country through hard times.

Lincoln Memorial

Washington Monument

Thomas Jefferson Memorial

People also visit Arlington National Cemetery and the Vietnam Veterans Memorial. These places honor men and women who have died for our country. There are many special places in our country's capital.

Arlington National Cemetery

Vietnam Veterans Memorial

What Do YOU Know?

1. Where does the President of the United States live?

2. How do we remember our country's great leaders?

Use a Map Grid

Maps help visitors to Washington, D.C., find routes to places they want to see. A **route** is a way to travel from one place to another. To help you find places, this map has a set of squares called a **grid**. Each grid square has a number and a letter.

1 Find the Lincoln Memorial. It is in square B-1. In which square is the Washington Monument?

2 In which square is the Vietnam Veterans Memorial?

3 What is in square E-5?

4 In which squares is the Reflecting Pool?

The Reflecting Pool

164

Washington, D.C.

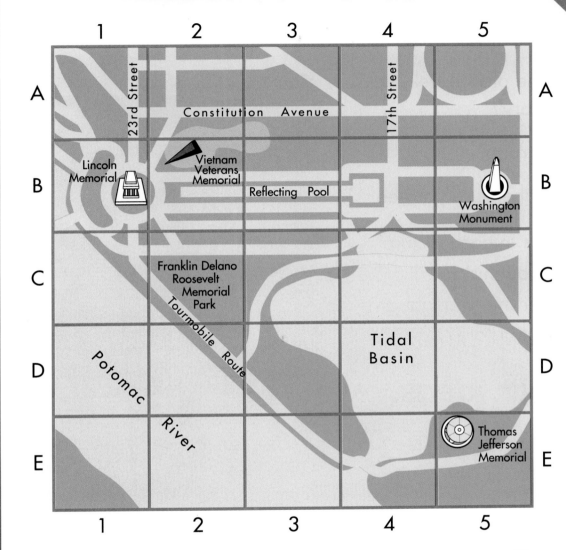

Think and Do

Follow a route. Put your finger in square E-5. Travel up to C-5. Go left to C-2. What park is in the center of the square?

165

History Clues

What can the pictures tell you about history?

Work with a group.

Make a list of the clues you see.

- What clues in each picture tell you about history?
- What other things might give clues about history?

Show your ideas.

Choose a way to show the class your ideas.

- Make up a story about the meaning of one of the clues.
- Role-play solving a history mystery.
- Draw a picture of another clue to history.

3

HENRY MORGENTHAU JR
SECRETARY OF THE TREASURY
JAMES A FARLEY
POSTMASTER GENERAL
LOUIS A SIMON
SUPERVISING ARCHITECT
GEORGE O VON NERTA
SUPERVISING ENGINEER
1934

4

5

6

JOHN
WOOD
MASSACHUSETTS
CPL
CONTINENTAL LINE
REVOLUTIONARY WAR
1753 - 1830

PIONEER WOMAN

American Portraits

A portrait is a picture or an interesting story about a person. Our country has many people to be proud of. Some are well known. Some are not. Look at and read portraits of seven Americans who have played a part in our history.

Thomas Edison

Some people have changed our lives with their new ideas. When you turn on a light, you can thank Thomas Edison. The electric lightbulb was his invention. An **invention** is a new kind of machine or a new way of doing something. Another of Edison's inventions was the phonograph. It led to the record player, and that led to the stereos and CD players we use today.

Dr. Charles Drew

You know that you can save your money in a bank. But did you know that blood can be saved in a different kind of bank? When Charles Drew was studying to be a doctor, he learned a lot about blood. He found a way to save blood so it could be used later. Now, when people get hurt and lose blood, saved blood can be used to make them well.

Dr. Drew's invention saved many soldiers' lives during a terrible war. Later he ran the Red Cross Blood Bank. His work is still saving people's lives today.

Susan B. Anthony

Some people speak out when laws are unfair. Susan B. Anthony spoke out. She was a teacher who said that our country's laws should be for all Americans. At that time, only men could vote. Her work helped change laws so that women could vote, too. Susan B. Anthony was the first woman shown on American money. Her picture is on the silver dollar.

Dr. Martin Luther King, Jr.

Dr. Martin Luther King, Jr., also worked to make things fair for all Americans. We honor his work with a holiday to celebrate his birthday.

Dr. King was a minister. He believed that people should not be treated differently because of their skin color. Dr. King was a great speaker. Many people followed his ideas for peaceful change. Later they were shocked and sad when Dr. King was shot. Today, people still remember his words.

Sequoyah

Many years ago, a Cherokee named Sequoyah wanted to help his people learn to read and write. But his people did not have an alphabet. So he made up one.

To show how his alphabet worked, Sequoyah wrote some words whispered to him by a stranger. Then he passed the paper to his daughter, Ahyoka, who read the words. The Cherokees were amazed at the "talking leaves." Sequoyah's alphabet was used to write a newspaper for his people. His great invention helped the Cherokees learn many new things.

History

𝘓
A

𝟰
B

Long, long ago people far away carved marks into clay and stone. Others drew pictures on a kind of paper called papyrus. Later, people called Phoenicians invented an alphabet like the one we use today. As they traveled to other places to trade, they taught writing to the people they met.

Arthur Dorros

Some people make a difference in our lives because we enjoy their music, art, or stories. Perhaps you have read <u>This Is My House</u>, <u>Abuela</u>, <u>Radio Man</u>, or <u>Isla</u>. These books were written by Arthur Dorros, who is also an artist. He uses both writing and drawing to show how he feels about people and places.

Arthur Dorros enjoys visiting classrooms and helping children find their own stories. He says, "Everyone has stories to tell." He believes that when you tell stories about the world, you can come to know it better. You can also learn more about yourself.

Kristi Yamaguchi

Some people do the kinds of things we wish we could do. In 1992, Kristi Yamaguchi won an Olympic gold medal for ice-skating.

When she was very young, Kristi had to wear special shoes to correct a problem with her feet. At age five, she was able to start skating. When she was eight, Kristi entered her first skating contest. Twelve years later, she was the best skater in the world!

Like the speaker in the poem "I Can!" Kristi Yamaguchi believes that children can do or be anything. They just need to have a dream and work hard.

What Do You Know?

1. Name someone who has made a difference in people's lives. What did he or she do?

2. Whose portrait would you add as an American to be proud of?

Play a Part in History

United States

Fort Wilkins, Michigan

The history museum at Fort Wilkins, Michigan, is a good place to learn about the past. Children 6 to 18 years old help in the museum. They are called Future Historians. The Future Historians dress in costumes and act like people who lived in Fort Wilkins more than one hundred years ago. To do this, they must learn what life was like at that time.

For three days in summer, the Future Historians go to camp. There they learn about the people who lived in Fort Wilkins around 1870. The children are given the names of real people they will pretend to be.

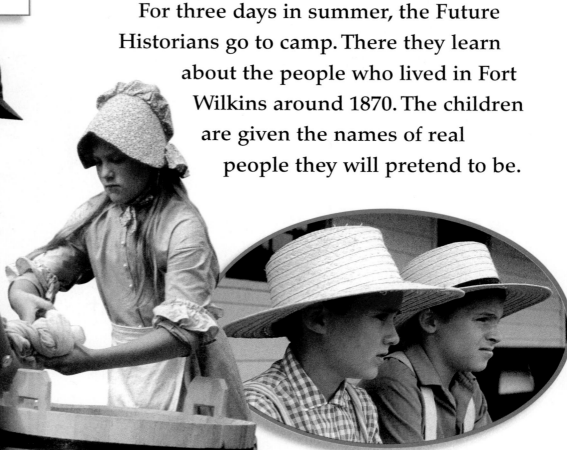

Old records and letters give them clues about these people. Old clothing, pictures, and tools tell even more.

The boys and girls have fun at camp. They try on the kinds of clothes people wore in 1870. They play games that children played in the past. They also play school the way school used to be.

The children are sorry when camp is over. But they are happy that they can now help at the museum. They are ready to play their parts and answer people's questions about the history of Fort Wilkins.

What Can You Do?

 Find out what your city, town, or area was like about a hundred years ago.

 Put on a play or plan an exhibit to share your community's history.

Visit the Internet at http://www.hbschool.com for additional resources.

Picture Summary

Follow the pictures. They will help you remember what you learned.

Talk About the Main Ideas

1 American Indians were the earliest people to live in our country.

2 Settlers from other countries built new homes in America.

3 Leaders have shaped our country's history.

4 Communities grow and change.

5 Many different people have helped make America great.

Write About a Hero Choose someone you are proud of. It may be someone you have read about or someone you know. Write about what that person has done. Tell what you can learn from your hero.

Use Vocabulary

Which word fits the sentence?

settler
invention
President
landmark
history

1 One way to learn about the past is to read _____ books.

2 You can read about _____ Abraham Lincoln.

3 You can learn about Thomas Edison's _____ of the lightbulb.

4 An American _____ had a hard life.

5 San Diego's lighthouse is a _____.

Check Understanding

1 How was the life of an American settler different from your life?

2 What can cause a community to change?

3 Who makes the laws for our country, and where do those people work?

4 Name an invention, and tell how it has changed people's lives.

Think Critically

1 What is history, and why do we study it?

2 Why are monuments and landmarks important to people in a community?

Use a Map Grid

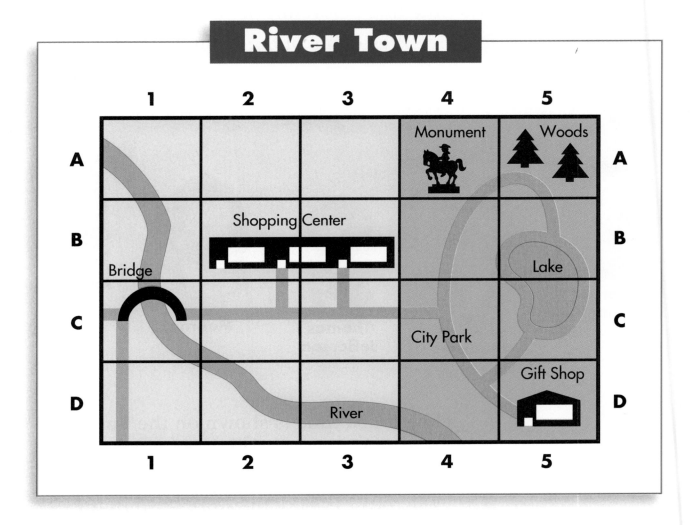

River Town

1. What building is in D-5?

2. In which square is the monument?

3. How many squares are between the park and the bridge?

Read a Time Line

The time line below shows the birthdays of the first five Presidents of the United States.

JAN | FEB | MAR | APR | MAY | JUN | JUL | AUG | SEP | OCT | NOV | DEC

George Washington

James Madison

Thomas Jefferson

James Monroe

John Adams

① How much time is shown on the time line?

② In what month was George Washington born?

③ Which two Presidents were born in the same month?

④ Abraham Lincoln was born on February 12, 1809. Where would you put his birthday?

Do It Yourself

Make a time line to show when people in your family have birthdays.

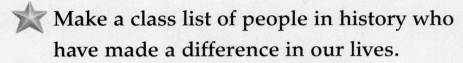

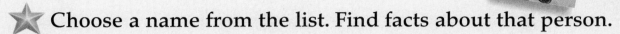

Make Who's Who Trading Cards

⭐ Make a class list of people in history who have made a difference in our lives.

⭐ Choose a name from the list. Find facts about that person.

⭐ Paste a picture of the person you chose on the front of an index card. On the back of the card, write when and where the person was born. Tell what he or she did.

⭐ Trade cards with your classmates.

HARCOURT BRACE

**Visit the Internet at
http://www.hbschool.com
for additional resources.**

Read More About It

Eleanor by Barbara Cooney. Viking. This story about Eleanor Roosevelt explains how she grew up to marry a President and help many people.

The Joke's on George by Michael O. Tunnell. Tambourine. George Washington visits a friend's museum.

Young Abe Lincoln by Cheryl Harness. National Geographic Society. Lincoln's boyhood on the American frontier prepared him to lead his country.

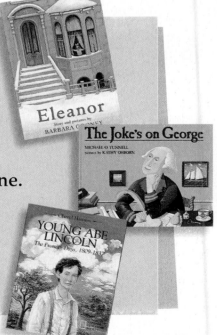

5

Being a Good Citizen

Vocabulary

vote
government
judge
mayor
freedom

vote

A choice that gets counted.

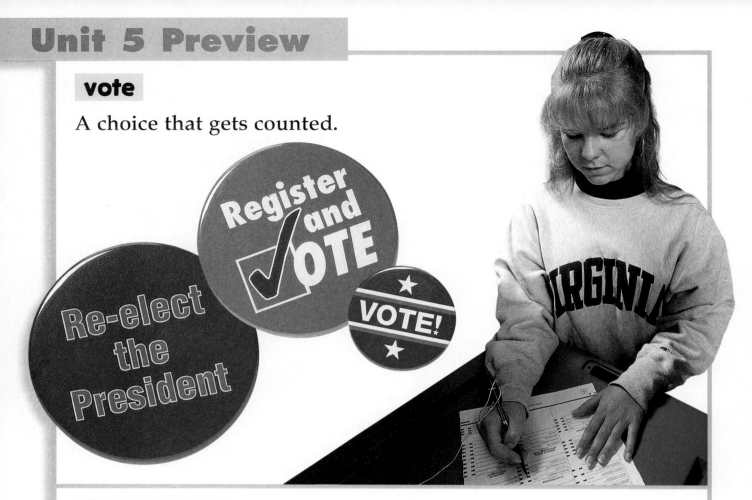

government

A group of people who make the
laws for a community or a country.

judge

Someone who works as a leader in court.

mayor

The leader of a city or town.

freedom

The right of people to make their own choices.

America

by Samuel F. Smith
illustrated by Byron Gin

My country, 'tis of thee,
Sweet land of liberty,
of thee I sing;
Land where my fathers died,
Land of the pilgrims' pride,
From every mountainside
Let freedom ring.

My native country, thee,
Land of the noble free,
Thy name I love;
I love thy rocks and rills,
Thy woods and templed hills;
My heart with rapture thrills
Like that above.

Proud Americans

Americans sing "America" on the Fourth of July. The Fourth of July is our country's birthday. Our community celebrates this special day, or **holiday**, with a parade. Did you know that the United States is more than 200 years old?

We like to honor our country during the school year, too. We decorate our room with balloons. We hang a banner with our country's motto, In God We Trust. A **motto** is a saying that people try to live by.

<u>E Pluribus Unum</u> is a motto that is on our money. The Latin words mean "out of many, one." We are one country of many different people.

Our country has many symbols. My class is making a bulletin board. We will show pictures of our country's symbols, such as the Statue of Liberty, the White House, and the bald eagle. One famous leader named Benjamin Franklin wanted the turkey to be America's bird. Our country's lawmakers chose the eagle instead.

Ms. Carroll's class is having a play. The children in the play are dressed as people in American history. They tell us about other American symbols.

I am Betsy Ross.

I sewed the first American flag. Our flag is red, white, and blue. Each star stands for one of the states in our country. The stripes stand for the first 13 states in the United States.

I am Francis Scott Key.

I wrote our country's anthem. An anthem is a song that honors something. The anthem of the United States is about the American flag. It is called "The Star-Spangled Banner."

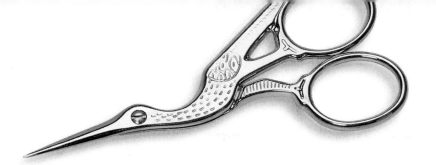

I am Thomas Jefferson.

In 1776 I wrote the Declaration of Independence that helped start the United States. People showed their love for the new country by ringing the Liberty Bell every Fourth of July. In 1835 the Liberty Bell cracked.

My name is George Washington.

I was the first President of the United States. You can see my picture and the Great Seal of the United States on a one-dollar bill. The Great Seal is on important papers, too.

What Do You Know?

1. What is our country's motto?
2. How do you show pride in your country?

Make a Choice by Voting

In our country, leaders like George Washington and Thomas Jefferson are chosen in an **election**. Here is how an election works.

Today is election day at Lincoln Elementary School. Each class will choose someone to send to a special student meeting. In an election, people **vote** to choose the person who will do a job for them.

One way to vote is to mark a piece of paper called a ballot. Each person may vote only once. How does the girl above show her choice? Why does she mark only one name on the ballot?

When people vote, they think about who will do the best job. What choice do these children have?

3

How will the children
decide who wins?

4

All voters agree to
accept the winner.

Think and Do

Make a list of the reasons you would
vote for someone in an election.

Our Country's Government

My class is learning about the people who make laws and lead our country. These groups of people are our **government**.

The Constitution is the highest law in our country. It protects all the people of the United States. The Constitution tells about the three branches, or parts, of our government. Each branch has its own job to do. We are making a mobile to show the branches of our government.

The President is in one branch of our government. The President leads our country. The President chooses people to help and to give advice. They work together in the White House. Do you know the name of our President?

Congress is another branch of government.
Members of Congress make new laws. These
lawmakers come from communities all over the
country. They vote for the laws they think we need.

The Supreme Court is also a branch of our government. It is the highest court in the United States. A court is where judges work. **Judges** tell us if laws are fair and decide if laws have been broken.

Parthenon

Supreme Court Building

The people of Greece built this temple more than 2,000 years ago. The Supreme Court is much newer. It was built in 1936. How does the Supreme Court building look like the Parthenon?

There are nine judges in the Supreme Court. They are called justices. Sandra Day O'Connor was the first woman to be a Supreme Court justice.

The President, the Congress, and the Supreme Court are in Washington, D.C. All three branches of the government work together to lead our country.

What Do You Know?

1. Who makes the laws in our country?

2. Why is it important to have good leaders?

The Supreme Court Justices

Ruth Bader Ginsburg

William H. Rehnquist

Anthony M. Kennedy

David H. Souter

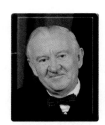

John Paul Stevens

Sandra Day O'Connor

Clarence Thomas

Stephen G. Breyer

Antonin Scalia

Find Capitals on a Map

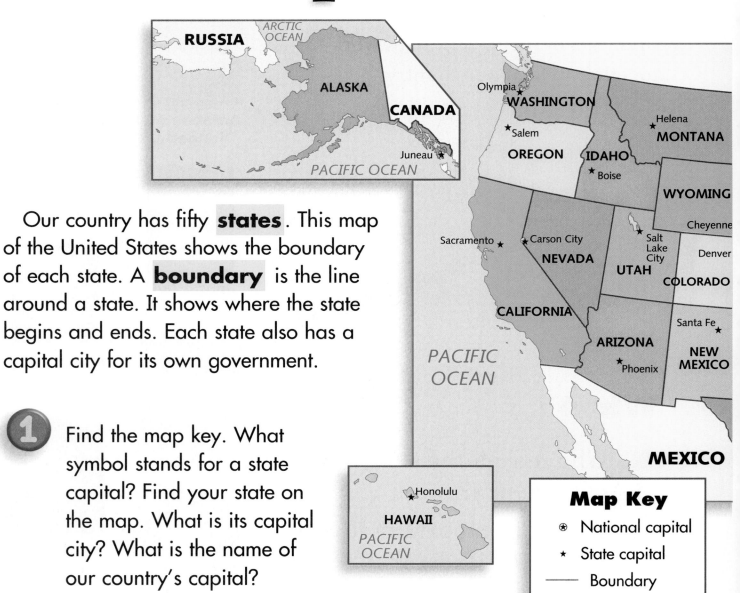

Our country has fifty **states**. This map of the United States shows the boundary of each state. A **boundary** is the line around a state. It shows where the state begins and ends. Each state also has a capital city for its own government.

1 Find the map key. What symbol stands for a state capital? Find your state on the map. What is its capital city? What is the name of our country's capital?

Map Key
- ⊛ National capital
- ★ State capital
- — Boundary

2 Find the compass rose at the bottom of the map. Remember, a compass rose gives the directions on a map.

3 Point to your state on the map. Tell what is north, south, east, and west of your state. What is the capital of each of your neighbor states?

United States

Think and Do

Find Georgia. What is the capital of the state that is west of Georgia?

Community Government

Citizens can work together to make changes.
Last year our school needed a new playground.
We wanted to use an empty lot near the school.
Maya's dad helped us write a letter. We asked our
teachers, parents, and neighbors to sign it.

1. This is the empty lot.

3. People signed the letter.

2. Maya's dad helped us write a letter.

Noel's mom gave the letter to the school board. The school board held a meeting. Many people came to the meeting to listen and speak. The school board voted to buy the empty lot.

Citizens worked together to build the playground. The mayor started the job. The **mayor** is one of our city leaders.

My teacher says we are lucky to live in the United States. Citizens can make changes in their schools, communities, states, and country.

4. The school board voted.

5. The mayor started the job.

What Do You Know?

1. Who are some community leaders?
2. How can you work with your leaders?

Understand What People Think

Not everyone in Maya and Noel's neighborhood wanted a new playground in the empty lot. Read this letter to the school board.

April 12, 1999

Dear Members of the School Board,

I live in the building next to an empty lot. The lot has been for sale for many months. I know that you want to buy it for a playground. I think that is a bad idea. Children make too much noise. I think they will also leave trash on the ground. I hope you will put your playground somewhere else. Thank you.

Sincerely,

John Wilson

People often have strong feelings about things. They want others to listen to their ideas. Sometimes they tell facts, or true statements. Sometimes they give opinions. Opinions tell what people think. People often have different opinions.

1 Read Mr. Wilson's letter. What does he feel strongly about?

2 What facts does he give about the empty lot?

3 What opinions does he have about children? How can you tell?

Think and Do

- Work with a partner.
- Write your own letter to the school board.
- Give two facts and two opinions about why the playground should be built on the empty lot.

Our Freedoms

People in our country have many freedoms. **Freedoms** are the rights people in the United States have to make their own choices. Patrick Henry was a famous leader who helped our country get its freedoms long ago. He loved freedom so much that he said, "Give me liberty or give me death!" Liberty is another word for freedom.

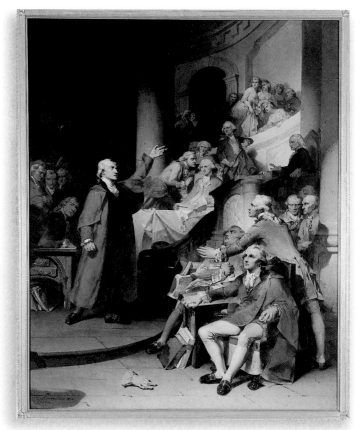

"Patrick Henry Before the Virginia House of Burgesses" by Peter F. Rothermel

Patrick Henry helped get the Bill of Rights added to the Constitution. The Bill of Rights lists the freedoms that Americans have.

Freedom of speech

Right to meet peacefully

Freedom of religion

Americans have enjoyed these freedoms for more than 200 years. The Constitution says that the government can never take them away.

Freedom of the press

Rosa Parks

Sometimes people help us remember what our freedoms are. A woman named Rosa Parks reminded us that the same freedoms belong to all Americans. Rosa Parks worked to help change things for African Americans. She said, "I was just one of many who fought for freedom."

Both Patrick Henry and Rosa Parks shared how they felt about freedom. Today many young people learn about their freedoms in school.

Rosa Parks grew up on her grandparents' farm in Alabama. As she became older, she saw that African Americans were not treated fairly. She did not think people should be kept apart by skin color. Later, she and her husband worked with groups to stop this. One day a bus driver said she must give up her seat to a white person. Rosa Parks would not do it. Unfair laws were changed because she believed in her freedom.

Our class made a banner to explain what freedoms mean to us. We all wrote on the banner. One girl wrote, "Freedom is having the same rules for everyone." Our banner was hung at City Hall for everyone to share.

What Do YOU Know?

1. Where is the Bill of Rights written?
2. What do our freedoms mean to you?

Getting Along

Work with a group. Talk about the children's different opinions.

- Why does each child think he or she is right?
- How can the children solve their problem?

What Would You Do?

Choose a way to show the class your ideas.

- Draw a cartoon.
- Act out your way to solve the problem.
- Write a story.

This is a boys' game. Go away.

Kids Voting USA

United States

Macon, Georgia

At Winship Magnet School in Macon, Georgia, children of all ages are learning how to be good citizens. They know that citizens must take an active part in their government.

Every year teachers Laney Sammons and Jeannie Waters work with second graders on activities that teach good citizenship. The children use ideas from a project called Kids Voting USA. They plan school elections, learn about their community government, and even go with their parents to vote on election day. Jeannie Webb Hodges, the principal at Winship, says "When the children talk about voting at home, their parents get excited, too."

As the children learn about voting, they also learn about finding information, solving problems, and making decisions. They have fun decorating their classrooms for voting day. In one classroom a life-size eagle reminds children of the symbols of the United States.

After the children vote, they wear their "I Voted" stickers proudly. With the voting habits they have learned, these young citizens will grow up to be active members of their community and country.

What Can You Do?

 Find out how citizens sign up to vote in your community.

 Make posters to remind people to vote.

 Visit the Internet at http://www.hbschool.com for additional resources.

Picture Summary

Look at the pictures. They will help you remember what you learned.

Talk About the Main Ideas

1. Americans honor their country and its history.

2. We elect people to be the leaders of our country.

3. The United States government has three branches.

4. States and communities have governments, too.

5. Americans have many freedoms.

Tell a Story Make up a story about a trip to our country's capital or your state's capital. Tell what you saw and who you met there.

I pledge Allegiance to the flag of the United States of America And to the Republic for which it stands, One Nation under God, Indivisible, with Liberty and Justice for all.

Use Vocabulary

Use the word in the box in your answer.

1. Is a **mayor** a leader of a city, state, or country?

2. Where does a **judge** work?

3. How many times can each person **vote** in an election?

4. How many branches does our country's **government** have?

5. What is one **freedom** Americans have?

Check Understanding

1. How do Americans honor their country?

2. What is the Constitution?

3. How does our government help us?

4. Who decides if laws are fair?

5. How do people help their government?

Think Critically

1. Do you think the bald eagle is a good symbol for our country? Explain.

2. Who are some leaders in your community?

3. What are some things that good citizens do?

Find Capitals on a Map

Five States

Map Key

★ State capital
— Boundary

1. Name two states that share a boundary.
2. What is the capital of Tennessee?
3. In which direction is Tennessee from Kentucky?
4. In which direction would you go to get from Richmond to Frankfort?

Do It Yourself

Make a map of your state and its neighbors.

Add the capitals.

Draw a compass rose.

Write two questions about finding capitals.

215

Apply Skills

Understand What People Think

1 Name something you have strong feelings about.

2 Give one fact and one opinion about the thing you named.

Make a Choice by Voting

In 1996 Massachusetts passed a law naming its state dessert. The idea for the law came from a group of school children. They wanted Boston cream pie to become the state dessert. Lawmakers voted—and agreed with their idea!

Work with your classmates to choose a snack for your state or city. Take a vote to decide the class favorite.

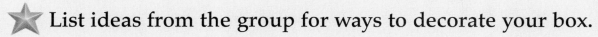

Unit Activity

Make Ballot Boxes

Work in small groups to make ballot boxes for all the classrooms in your school.

⭐ List ideas from the group for ways to decorate your box.

⭐ Vote to decide which idea or ideas to use.

⭐ List the jobs that need to be done and who will do them.

⭐ Give your box to another class. Tell them what your class has learned about voting.

Visit the Internet at
http://www.hbschool.com
for additional resources.

Read More About It

<u>Billy the Great</u> by Rosa Guy. Delacorte. Two families find a way to work out their problems and become good neighbors.

<u>The Flag We Love</u> by Pam Muñoz Ryan. Charlesbridge. This poem explains the meaning of the flag through our history.

<u>A Very Important Day</u> by Maggie Rugg Herold. Morrow. On a snowy day in New York, 219 people from 32 countries become new American citizens.

217

Vocabulary

pioneer

ancestor

custom

artifact

communication

pioneer

A person who first settles in a new place.

ancestor

Someone in a family who lived long ago.

custom

A way of doing something.

artifact

An object that is made and used by people.

communication

Sharing ideas with others.

Pride

by Alma Flor Ada
illustrated by Gerardo Suzan

Proud of my family
proud of my language
proud of my culture
proud of my race
proud to be who I am.

Orgullo

por Alma Flor Ada
ilustrado por Gerardo Suzan

Orgullosa de mi familia
Orgullosa de mi idioma
Orgullosa de mi cultura
Orgullosa de mi raza
Orgullosa de ser quien soy.

People on the Move

Remember that settlers came to live in America long ago. People from Spain settled in the West. English settlers built communities in the East. There was a lot of land in between that was not settled.

Then people from the East began to move across the country as pioneers. A **pioneer** is a person who first settles in a new place. The pioneers traveled on foot, on horseback, and in wagons. They crossed rivers, plains, and mountains. They started farms and ranches and built towns all across the land.

"Pioneers of the West" by Helen Lundeberg

224

More pioneers moved across the country. Soon trains brought the things that the communities needed. They also brought more people.

Some people started businesses. Communities built schools and churches. Some towns grew into cities. In time every part of the country was settled, from the Atlantic Ocean to the Pacific Ocean.

The first railroad to cross the country was built 130 years ago. One group of workers started from Sacramento, California. Another group started from Omaha, Nebraska. The tracks met in Promontory, Utah. Now people could travel by train all the way across the continent.

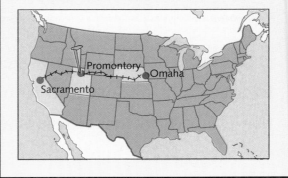

Many people moved from place to place in the United States. People also came from other places around the world to live in this new country. They sailed here on big ships. In the East the ships landed at Ellis Island. In the West they landed at Angel Island.

In both places the new people had to tell why they wanted to move to the United States. Doctors also made sure they were healthy.

Read what some children thought about coming to a strange new land.

Ellis Island

Golda Meir from Russia

"Going to America then was almost like going to the moon. We were all bound for places about which we knew nothing at all and for a country that was totally strange to us."

Eleven-year-old from Turkey

"I couldn't read, I couldn't write, I couldn't speak. I had never been to school in my life until I came here, on account of the war over there. But I picked it up. I picked it up very good, thank God."

Helen Cohen from Poland

"When I was about 10 years old I said, 'I have to go to America.' I was dreaming about it. And I was dreaming, and my dream came true. When I came here, I was in a different world. I'm free. I'm just like a bird. You can fly and land on any tree and you're free."

What Do You Know?

1. How did the pioneers travel across America?

2. How would you feel about moving to another country?

WINTER DAYS
IN THE
BIG WOODS

by Laura Ingalls Wilder
illustrated by Renée Graef

Once upon a time, a little girl named Laura lived in the Big Woods of Wisconsin in a little house made of logs.

Laura lived in the little house with her Pa, her Ma, her big sister Mary, her baby sister Carrie, and their good old bulldog Jack.

Winter was coming to the Big Woods. Soon the little house would be covered with snow. Pa went hunting every day so that they would have meat during the long, cold winter.

Ma, Laura, and Mary gathered potatoes and carrots, beets and turnips, cabbages and onions, and peppers and pumpkins from the garden next to the little house.

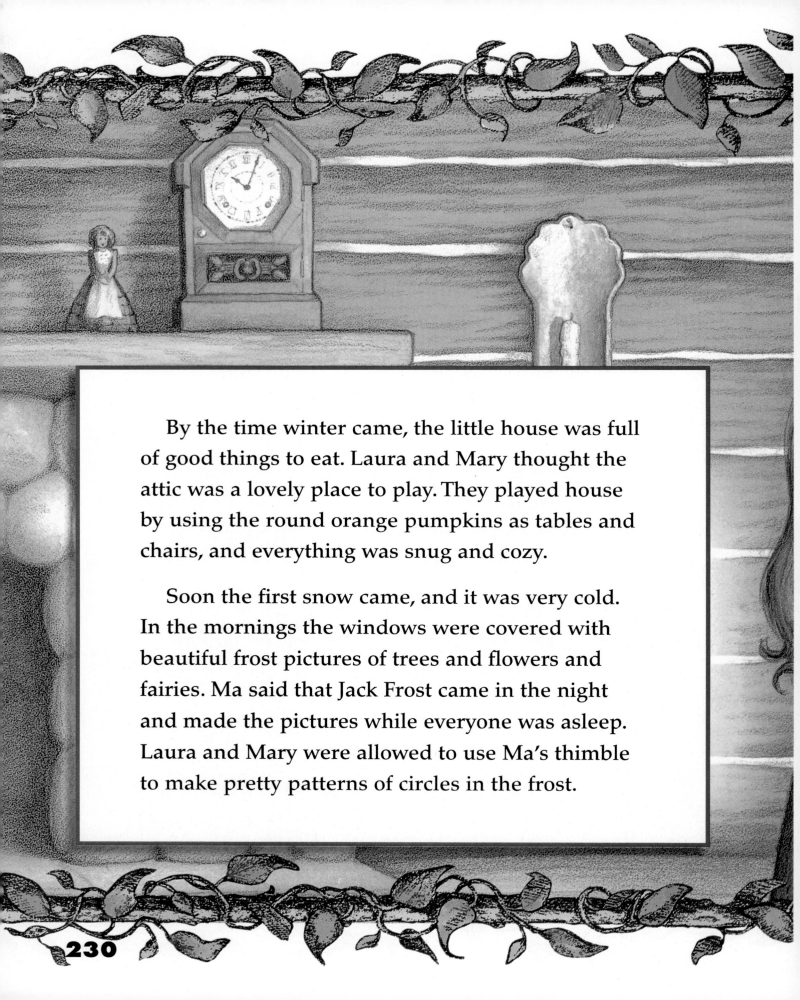

By the time winter came, the little house was full of good things to eat. Laura and Mary thought the attic was a lovely place to play. They played house by using the round orange pumpkins as tables and chairs, and everything was snug and cozy.

Soon the first snow came, and it was very cold. In the mornings the windows were covered with beautiful frost pictures of trees and flowers and fairies. Ma said that Jack Frost came in the night and made the pictures while everyone was asleep. Laura and Mary were allowed to use Ma's thimble to make pretty patterns of circles in the frost.

In the mornings Laura and Mary helped Ma wash the dishes and make the beds. After this was done, Ma began the work that belonged to that day. Each day had its own proper work. Ma would say:

Wash on Monday,
Iron on Tuesday,
Mend on Wednesday,
Churn on Thursday,
Clean on Friday,
Bake on Saturday,
Rest on Sunday.

Laura liked the churning and baking days best of all. Ma had to churn the cream for a long time until it turned into butter. Mary could sometimes churn while Ma rested, but Laura was too little.

On Saturdays, when Ma made the bread, Laura and Mary each had a little piece of dough to make into a little loaf. Ma even gave them a bit of cookie dough to make little cookies.

After the day's work was done, Ma would sometimes cut out paper dolls for Laura and Mary. She drew their faces on with a pencil, and cut dresses, hats, and ribbons out of colored paper so that Mary and Laura could dress their dolls beautifully.

But the best time of all was at night, when Pa came home. He would throw off his fur cap and coat and mittens and call, "Where's my little half-pint of sweet cider half drunk up?" That was Laura, because she was so small.

Sometimes Pa would take down his fiddle and sing. Pa would keep time with his foot. Laura and Mary would clap their hands to the music when he sang:

"Yankee Doodle went to town,
He wore his striped trousies,
He swore he couldn't see the town,
There was so many houses."

Other times Pa would tell stories. When Laura and Mary begged him for a story, he would take them on his knees and tickle their faces with his long whiskers until they laughed out loud. His eyes were blue and merry.

Outside it was cold and snowy, but the little log cabin was snug and cozy. Pa, Ma, Laura, Mary, and Baby Carrie were comfortable and happy in their little house in the Big Woods.

What Do You Know?

What did Laura's family do for fun?

A World of People

Many people come from other countries to live in the United States. Join these children as they meet a new friend. See what they learn about him and about one another.

Today we have a special visitor in our classroom. His name is Antonio. He is from Italy. Antonio has brought pictures of his family and his school. He likes to read books, just as we do. His books are written in the Italian language. Antonio is learning to speak English. He plays his violin for us because music is a language we can all understand.

Antonio is Tina's cousin. Tina's ancestors came from Italy. **Ancestors** are people in our families who lived before us. The ancestors of many Americans came from other countries. Some of them moved here hundreds of years ago. Others have been here only a short time.

Chad's ancestors came here from Africa long ago. Emily's family moved here from Poland when she was a baby. Cam Linh and her family just moved here from Vietnam.

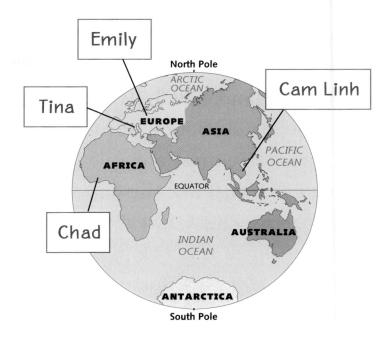

Our class is making a quilt. We have made patches that tell about our families. Mine shows Grandma, me, and my bicycle. Grandma is from Ireland, so I drew a shamrock on my patch. Bobby is from Canada. He drew a maple leaf on his patch, just like the one on the Canadian flag. Carla's patch has ballet shoes and a Hopi Indian design. Her ancestors were some of the first Americans.

Our teacher says the United States is like a big quilt. Each patch is different, but together the pieces are strong and beautiful.

Our quilt helps us know more about one another. That makes it easier to be friends.

What Do You Know?

1. Where do many Americans' ancestors come from?

2. Why is it important to learn about other people?

243

Use a Bar Graph

Our class quilt tells about our ancestors. We also made a bar graph to show how many of our ancestors came from each part of the world. A **bar graph** is a kind of drawing that shows numbers of things.

1 Look at the bar graph. The children listed the continents their ancestors came from. Why do you think they added <u>Not Sure</u>?

2 Find Africa on the graph. What number does the bar reach? How many children have ancestors from Africa?

3 Four children have ancestors from the same continent. Which continent is that?

4 Compare the bars. From which continent did the most ancestors come? From which continent did the fewest come?

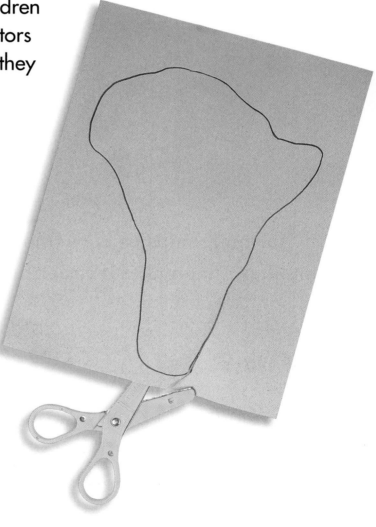

244

Our Ancestors

	0	1	2	3	4	5	6	7
Africa								
Asia								
North America								
South America								
Europe								
Australia								
Not Sure								

Think and Do

Work with classmates to make a bar graph. List foods from different countries. Then use the bars to show the number of children who like each food.

A Family History

Every family has a history. Babies are born, and then they grow up. As grown-ups they may marry and have children of their own. Some people move far away to live in another part of the world. Others stay in the same place all their lives. Each family has a past. Every family has a story to tell.

Seven-year-old Bryan Chiang was born near San Francisco, California. He has lived in the same house all his life. His grandparents, who live near him, were born in China. They moved to the United States a long time ago to find a better life.

Bryan Chiang and his family in Chinatown

When Bryan visits his grandparents' house, he can see things that came from China. He likes to use the abacus. People in China have used this tool for thousands of years. With it they can add, subtract, multiply, and divide without using a pencil and paper.

Bryan's grandfather learned to use an abacus when he was Bryan's age. Later he brought the abacus with him to the United States. For many years he used it in his business to add up his customers' bills.

Bryan's grandfather explains how an abacus works.

Bryan's father works in a bank. He uses a computer.

Sometimes Bryan's grandparents show him photographs from China. Many of these show family members who lived a long time ago. He sees pictures of his great-grandparents and of his grandparents when they were young.

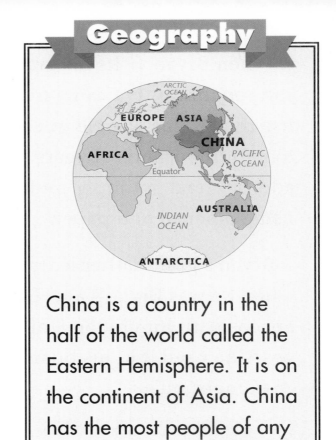

China is a country in the half of the world called the Eastern Hemisphere. It is on the continent of Asia. China has the most people of any country in the world—more than one billion.

The photographs from China help Bryan understand his family history.

One way people learn about their family history is by making a family tree. A family tree is a drawing that shows family members, their parents' family members, and so on over many years.

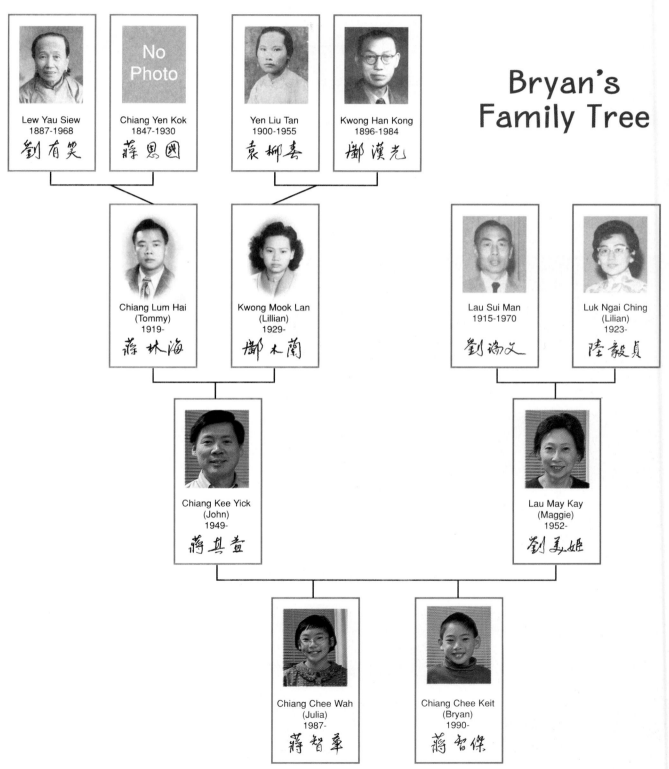

Bryan's Family Tree

Lew Yau Siew
1887-1968
劉有笑

Chiang Yen Kok
1847-1930
蔣恩國

Yen Liu Tan
1900-1955
袁柳春

Kwong Han Kong
1896-1984
鄺漢光

Chiang Lum Hai
(Tommy)
1919-
蔣林海

Kwong Mook Lan
(Lillian)
1929-
鄺木蘭

Lau Sui Man
1915-1970
劉瑞文

Luk Ngai Ching
(Lilian)
1923-
陸毅貞

Chiang Kee Yick
(John)
1949-
蔣其益

Lau May Kay
(Maggie)
1952-
劉美姬

Chiang Chee Wah
(Julia)
1987-
蔣智華

Chiang Chee Keit
(Bryan)
1990-
蔣智傑

Bryan loves to eat Chinese food. Sometimes his grandfather lets him help make a meal. When Bryan's father was a boy, his grandfather taught him to cook. Now Bryan's grandfather is teaching Bryan how to make wonton soup, one of Bryan's favorite foods. Bryan says, "My grandpa is a good teacher as well as a good cook."

To make wonton for the soup, Bryan puts meat filling in the center of a piece of dough. Then he wets the edges of the dough, folds them over the filling, and presses them together.

Bryan carefully pinches the wonton to keep the filling inside.

Bryan is proud of his Chinese background. He and his sister, Julia, are learning to speak Chinese. Bryan and Julia can write their names in Chinese letters called characters. They have learned many things about their family's history.

Bryan likes to think about how his family tree first started to grow, far away in China. Now the tree is larger, with branches in the United States, too. He wonders how big his family tree will grow in the future.

What Do You Know?

1. Where did Bryan's grandparents come from?

2. What can you learn from your grandparents?

Community Celebrations

In some communities, families celebrate special holidays. They may wear colorful costumes and eat tasty foods. They may dance and sing songs passed down from their ancestors. Our class made a scrapbook of some of these special times.

Chinese New Year

For several days during Chinese New Year, people wish each other "Gung Hay Fat Choy" or "Happy New Year." You can see bright-red decorations everywhere. People eat spring rolls and duck with rice stuffing. These are old Chinese customs. A **custom** is the way people usually do things.

Another favorite custom is carrying paper lanterns through the streets behind a dancing dragon.

Cinco de mayo

On May 5, Mexican Americans watch parades with riders on beautiful horses. The smell of tortillas, burritos, and tamales fills the air. This is Cinco de mayo. It is a fiesta, or feast, that reminds us of the freedom Mexicans fought for long ago.

Everyone loves dancing and singing to the music of the guitars and horns. Children have fun trying to break piñatas. The piñatas are stuffed with fruits, candies, and toys.

Kwanzaa

At the end of December, many African American families celebrate Kwanzaa. On each of the seven days, a candle is lit. The first day is Umoja, which means unity, or togetherness.

Kuumba is the sixth day. People wear colorful African clothing, tell old stories, and dance to African drums.

The last day is the Karamu, or feast. Black-eyed peas, ham, apple salad, corn bread, sweet-potato pie, and other delicious dishes are served.

Juneteenth

Some African Americans celebrate another holiday called Juneteenth. On June 19 they remember the day in 1865 when slaves in Texas were given their freedom. Families gather at parades and picnics to tell stories about their history. Many people give thanks for their freedom by singing the hymn "Lift Ev'ry Voice."

"Lift ev'ry voice and sing
Till earth and heaven ring,
Ring with the harmonies of Liberty."

Greek Epiphany

For almost 100 years Greeks in Tarpon Springs, Florida, have celebrated the Feast of the Epiphany. January 6 is an important holiday of the Greek church. Families parade from the church to Spring Bayou for the blessing of the water. A cross is thrown into the water, and young men dive after it. The one who finds it wins honor.

A glendi, or festival, follows with dancing and music and plenty of seafood to eat. Thousands of visitors come to Tarpon Springs every year for this exciting Greek festival.

What Do You Know?

1. What group celebrates Kwanzaa?
2. How does your family or community celebrate special times?

Learn from Artifacts

Celebrations are important to Native American people, too. The objects in the photos were made to be used in celebrations. Objects made by people are called **artifacts**. Artifacts help us learn about the lives of the people who make them.

1 Look at the artifacts and read about them. Describe each artifact. How do you think each one is used?

2 What materials do the Indians use to make the objects?

3 What can you tell about the Hopis by looking at the kachina doll?

4 What can you tell about the Plains Indians from their artifact?

The Hopis carve kachina dolls from wood to teach children the ways of their people.

The Plains Indians use rattles made from gourds to celebrate good harvests.

The Navajos believe sand paintings help sick people in healing ceremonies.

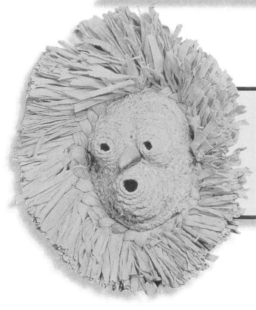

Cornhusk masks are used by the Iroquois in celebrations.

Some Indians of the Northwest Coast honor their ancestors with totem poles carved from tree trunks.

Think and Do

Draw a picture of an artifact that might tell someone about you.

257

LESSON 6

One for All, All for One

People around the world have many of the same needs. They share the same feelings about what makes life good. People everywhere think about how to keep safe and healthy and how to get along with others.

Some children in other countries made posters to show how to keep our world a good place to live. How are their ideas like yours?

Henrik Kaurin
Age 8
Sweden

Use the earth as you need it.

PEACE IS Good BECAUSE HOMES don't get deotroyed.

Mirna Hamady
Age 8
Abu Dhabi,
United Arab
Emirates

Daniel Vargas
Age 7
Costa Rica

We have to keep the water clean.

259

Kevyn Loggins
Age 7
Germany

Peace is at my friend's house. She lets me hold her ♥ rabbit and I say thank you very much. Friendship makes peace.

Natalie Madi
Age 6
Lebanon

Peace begins with me by playing nicely in the game.

Reuse or recycle.

John Oh
Age 7
South Korea

The children made these posters to communicate their feelings. **Communication** is the sharing of ideas. When people get to know one another, they can work together to solve problems.

What Do You Know?

1. Name a problem children around the world care about.

2. What are some ways people communicate with each other?

Act on Your Own

Many children are interested in helping their communities. When Kristina Swartwout was nine years old, she saw a problem in her town of Ashland, Oregon. Cars were not stopping for children at crosswalks. Kristina wrote a letter to the Ashland newspaper. The mayor of Ashland read the letter and made Kristina a member of the Traffic Safety Commission.

Acting on your own is showing **independence**. Kristina's independent act helped make her community safer for everyone.

Dear Editor,

Kristina followed these steps:

1 Name the problem. → Children cannot cross the street safely.

2 Decide what you want to do. → Let people know about the problem.

3 Think of ways to act on your own to solve the problem. → Write a letter to the newspaper or make posters.

4 Think about what might happen. → Many people might read the letter. Fewer people might see the posters.

5 Choose the best way to solve the problem. → Write a letter to the newspaper.

Think and Do

Think of a problem and write a plan for solving it.

Prairie Peace Park

United States

Lincoln,
Nebraska

Long ago, wagon trains carried settlers from many countries across the prairies of the United States. Today, people from around the world come together outside Lincoln, Nebraska, at Prairie Peace Park. Here children can discover how important it is to get along with our world neighbors.

In the Children's Maze, ideas for a safe and peaceful world are found in paintings from children around the world. As visitors walk through the maze, they can use rubber stamps to show that they reached each of the ten stations.

Children's
Maze

264

In Children's Sculptures, visitors can see the sixteen winning sculptures from the Children's Peace Statue Project. The sculptures give meaning to the park's motto Where Children's Visions Come to Life.

Also interesting is the World Peace Mural. Artists from 29 nations carved the mural, which is made from clay marked by the footprints of one thousand people.

Prairie Peace Park has more mazes, maps to walk on, videos, and computer games for all to enjoy. Children can also go to Peace Camp there. The park's director, Don Tilley, and his volunteers say, "Give children the right view of the world, and they will give us peace."

What Can You Do?

⭐ Make a peace mural for your school.

⭐ Talk to people from other countries to find out who they are and what they care about.

 Visit the Internet at http://www.hbschool.com for additional resources.

Picture Summary

Look at the pictures. They will help you remember what you learned.

Talk About the Main Ideas

1 People have moved from place to place in our country.

2 People from many different countries live in the United States.

3 People find out about themselves by learning their family history.

4 Groups of people celebrate holidays with special customs.

5 People everywhere care about peace, cooperation, and a healthy world.

Make Puppets Make a stick puppet of someone in your family or someone you know. Then work with a partner. Use your puppets to describe a family custom or an interesting fact about the family.

266

Use Vocabulary

Give another example to help explain each word.

Word	Examples	
1. custom	Fourth of July parade	
2. pioneer	an explorer	
3. artifact	an old cooking pot	
4. ancestor	great-grandmother	
5. communication	writing a letter	

Check Understanding

1 How did pioneers help our country grow?

2 The ancestors of Americans came from many countries. Name three of these countries.

3 How do families share their history?

4 What can we learn about people from their holidays?

5 Why do people need to communicate?

Think Critically

How is America like a big quilt? How does that make America strong?

Use a Bar Graph

The bar graph shows how many children would like to visit each place.

Places We Would Like to Visit

	0	1	2	3	4	5	6	7
Animal Park in Africa								
Castles in Europe								
Rain Forest in South America								
Kangaroo Ranch in Australia								

1. What choices did the children have?

2. Which place was chosen by the most children?

3. Which place was chosen by the fewest children?

Do It Yourself

Make a bar graph to show how long families have lived in your community. Ask classmates to find out when their families first moved to your area. Make bars to show less than 10 years, 20 years, 30 years, 40 years, and more than 50 years.

269

Learn from Artifacts

What might you learn from looking at this arrowhead?

What might you learn from looking at this washboard?

Choose one of the artifacts above.
Work with a partner to find answers to these questions about your artifact.

• How was it made?

• How was it used?

• What does it tell you about the user?

• How is it like something you know about today?

Tell about something you use today that may be called an artifact in the future.

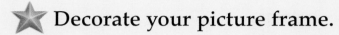

Unit Activity

Make a Picture Frame

⭐ Glue craftsticks together to make a picture frame.

⭐ Decorate your picture frame.

⭐ Ask for a photograph or draw a picture of your family or a relative. Tape it to the picture frame.

⭐ Make a name and date tag to tape to the back of the picture. Hang your picture at home.

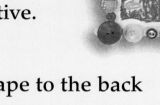

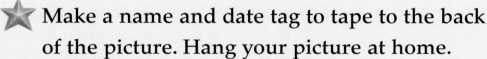

HARCOURT BRACE

Visit the Internet at
http://www.hbschool.com
for additional resources.

Read More About It

<u>The New Land, A First Year on the Prairie</u> by Marilynn Reynolds. Orca. The author describes her grandparents' pioneer life.

<u>Family Pictures</u> by Carmen Lomas Garza. Children's Book Press. An artist paints and writes about family customs.

<u>The Keeping Quilt</u> by Patricia Polacco. Simon & Schuster. A homemade quilt is handed down in a Jewish family.

Glossary

A

ancestor

Someone in a family who lived long ago. My **ancestor** came to America from England. (page 241)

artifact

An object that is made and used by people. This bowl is an Indian **artifact**. (page 256)

B

Family Trips

bar graph

A picture that shows how many or how much. This **bar graph** shows the states one family has visited. (page 244)

boundary

A line that shows where one state ends and another begins. The red line shows the **boundary** between Indiana and Ohio. (page 198)

business

A place where people make or sell goods or give services. My family started a TV repair **business**. (page 128)

C

capital

A city in which government leaders meet and work. Washington, D.C., is the **capital** of the United States. (page 160)

cause

A person or thing that makes something happen. Lightning was the **cause** of the fire. (page 158)

citizen

A member of a community. Pedro is a **citizen** of the United States. (page 32)

city

A large community where people live and work. New York City is the largest **city** in the United States. (page 24)

compass rose

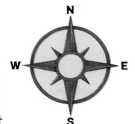

Arrows on a map that show directions. The **compass rose** shows which way is north, south, east, and west. (page 28)

colony

A place that is ruled by another country. Virginia was the first English **colony** in America. (page 152)

Congress

Our country's lawmakers. The **Congress** of the United States meets in the Capitol Building. (page 161)

communication

Sharing ideas with others. Many people use telephones for **communication**. (page 261)

conservation

Working to save resources or make them last longer. Forest rangers teach us about the **conservation** of trees. (page 86)

community

A place where people live and the people who live there. The **community** I live in is a big city. (page 21)

consumer

A person who buys and uses goods and services. This **consumer** is buying food for a picnic. (page 119)

continent

One of the largest bodies of land on the Earth. We live on the **continent** of North America. (page 60)

country

A land and the people who live in that land. The United States is one of three **countries** in North America. (page 32)

crop

A kind of plant that people grow for food or other uses. Corn is an important **crop** in the United States. (page 63)

custom

A way of doing something. Eating with chopsticks is a **custom** in many Asian countries. (page 252)

D

desert

A dry place. Very little rain falls in a **desert**. (page 51)

diagram

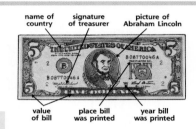

A drawing that shows the parts of something. The **diagram** shows the parts of a five-dollar bill. (page 126)

direction

North, south, east, or west. The sign tells us in which **direction** to go. (page 28)

E

effect

Something that happens from a cause. The forest fire was the **effect** of a lightning strike. (page 158)

election

The time when people vote. The **election** for President is held in November. (page 192)

freedom

The right of people to make their own choices. Americans have the **freedom** to worship as they please. (page 204)

equator

A line on a map or globe that is halfway between the North Pole and the South Pole. The weather at the **equator** is hot. (page 61)

geography

The study of the Earth and its people. Maps show something about the **geography** of a place. (page 48)

factory

A place where people make goods. This **factory** makes shoes. (page 108)

globe

A model of the Earth. We find places on our classroom **globe**. (page 60)

flow chart

A chart that shows the order in which things happen. The **flow chart** shows how to make a kite. (page 66)

goods

Things that people make or grow. People who play soccer buy these **goods**. (page 26)

government

A group of people who make the laws for a community or a country. There are people from each state in the United States **government**. (page 194)

grid

Lines that cross one another to form boxes. The lines of a **grid** can help you find places on a map. (page 164)

group

A number of people doing an activity together. This **group** is making music. (page 14)

history

The story of what has happened in a place. This picture book is about the **history** of our country. (page 142)

holiday

A time to celebrate. The Fourth of July is an American **holiday**. (page 188)

income

The money people earn for the work they do. I am saving part of my **income** to buy a computer. (page 122)

independence

The freedom of people to choose their own government and make their own laws. On the Fourth of July, we celebrate our country's **independence**. (page 262)

invention

Something that has been made for the first time. The first lightbulb was an important **invention**. (page 168)

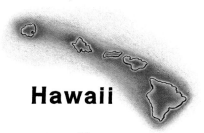

island

Land that has water all around it. The state of Hawaii is made up of many **islands**. (page 52)

landmark

A familiar object at a place. The Alamo is a Texas **landmark**. (page 157)

judge

Someone who works as a leader in court. The **judge** ruled that Mrs. Page had broken the law. (page 196)

law

A rule that everyone must follow. The **law** says cars must stop at a stop sign. (page 25)

lake

A body of water that has land all around it. The people who live around the lake enjoy fishing. (page 53)

lawmaker

A leader who makes laws. Many **lawmakers** work in our state capital. (page 161)

landform

A kind of land. Mountains, hills, and plains are **landforms**. (page 50)

leader

A person who helps a group plan what to do. A principal is the **leader** of a school. (page 16)

M

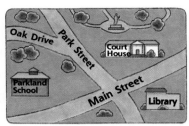

map
A drawing that shows where places are. We can find the library on the **map**. (page 23)

motto
A word or short saying that tells a feeling or an idea. Our country's **motto** is "In God We Trust." (page 188)

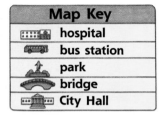

map key
A list of the symbols on a map. The **map key** tells what the symbols on a map stand for. (page 28)

mountain
The highest kind of land. There is snow on these **mountains**. (page 50)

mayor
The leader of a city or a town. The **mayor** meets with the lawmakers of our community. (page 201)

N

needs
Things people cannot live without. Food, clothing, and a place to live are **needs**. (page 18)

monument
Something set up to honor someone or something. This **monument** honors George Washington. (page 162)

neighborhood
A small part of a community. Our **neighborhood** has a fruit and vegetable market. (page 18)

ocean

A very large body of salty water. The Pacific **Ocean** is west of the United States. (page 52)

pollution

Anything that makes the air, land, or water unclean. Throwing garbage into a lake or river causes **pollution**. (page 90)

pictograph

A picture that uses symbols to show numbers of things. This **pictograph** shows how the children in one class come to school. (page 106)

prediction

Something a person says will happen. Tom's **prediction** is that it is going to rain. (page 113)

pioneer

A person who leads the way into land that has not been settled. Many **pioneers** traveled west in covered wagons. (page 224)

President

The leader of the United States. George Washington was our country's first **President**. (page 160)

plain

Land that is mostly flat. Our farm is on a **plain**. (page 51)

producer

A person who makes or grows something. Factory and farm workers are **producers**. (page 118)

R

resource

Something people use that comes from the Earth. Wood is an important **resource**. (page 71)

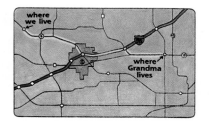

river

A long body of water that flows through the land. The Mississippi River is the longest **river** in the United States. (page 53)

route

A way to go from one place to another. The map shows the **route** to Grandma's house. (page 164)

rule

Something you must or must not do. A good **rule** for home and school is "Put things away after using them." (page 16)

S

services

Jobs people do that help others. Firefighters, police officers, and teachers provide **services**. (page 27)

settler

A person who makes a home in a new place. **Settlers** from many countries built homes in the West. (page 148)

shelter

A place to live. Some American Indians built their **shelters** from clay. (page 142)

California

state

A part of our country. The United States has fifty **states**. (page 198)

suburb

A community near a city. We live in a **suburb** of Chicago. (page 49)

symbol

A picture that stands for something real. A square is a **symbol** for a store on this map. (page 28)

T

table

Lists of things in groups. This **table** shows my best friends. (page 82)

taxes

Money people pay to their government for services. This man's **taxes** will pay for community services. (page 104)

time line

A line that shows when things happened. This **time line** shows when Fred took trips this year. (page 146)

trade

To give money, goods, or services to get something in return. Mary wants to **trade** her book for Nancy's. (page 114)

transportation

Any way of moving people or things from place to place. Airplanes are one kind of **transportation**. (page 114)

V

valley

Low land between hills or mountains. A small river runs through the **valley**. (page 50)

vote

A choice that gets counted. The person who gets the most **votes** is the winner. (page 192)

W

wants

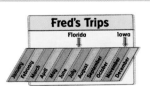

Things people would like to have. A new car is one of my family's **wants**. (page 122)

Credits

Photo Credits:
Key: (t) top; (b) bottom; (l) left; (r) right; (c) center
Table of Contents:
iii: Rich Franco/HBC; iv: John Elk/Tony Stone Images; v: Mark Robinson/The Biz Kids Store; vi: Superstock; vii: Rich Franco/HBC; viii: Bob Daemmrich

Unit 1:
8(bl): Superstock; 8-9: Lillian Gee/Picture It; 10 (tr): HBC; 10 (bl): Superstock; 10 (tl): Bob Daemmrich/Stock Boston; 10 (tc): Fran Antmann; 11 (tc): HBC; 11 (tr): Gabe Palmer/Stock Market; 11 (br): John Scheiber/Stock Market; 11 (tl): Michal Heron/Stock Market; 11 (bl): Tom Tracy/Stock Market; 15 (tr): Michael Groen Photography; 15 & 16: Rich Franco/HBC; 16 (l): Corbis/Bettmann; 16-17: Rich Franco/HBC; 18-19: Lillian Gee/Picture It; 19 (tr): Lawrence Migdale; 19 (br): Michael Groen Photography; 20 (b): Lawrence Midgale; 20 (t): Lillian Gee/Picture It; 21 (tr): Superstock; 21 (tc): David Young-Wolff/PhotoEdit; 21 (tl): Don Smetzer/Tony Stone Images; 21 (br): Myrleen Ferguson/PhotoEdit; 22: Alex MacLean /Landslides; 24 (bl): Superstock; 24 (br): Superstock; 24 (tl): Richard Haynes/HBC; 24-25: Michael Groen Photography; 25 (tl & tr): Superstock; 25 (br): David Simson/Stock Boston; 26 (tl): Owen Frank/Stock Boston; 26 (bl): Richard Haynes/HBC; 26-27 (b): Richard Haynes/HBC; 27 (tr): Richard Haynes/HBC; 32 (t): Andy Sacks/Tony Stone Images; 32 (b): Lawrence Migdale/Stock Boston; 32 (bc): Victoria Bowen/HBC; 33 (cr): Bob Daemmrich; 33 (tl): C. Frank Crzus/FPG; 33 (bcr): Dennis MacDonald/PhotoEdit; 33 (tcr): Paul Conklin/PhotoEdit; 33 (tr): Prettyman/PhotoEdit; 33 (bcl): Robert Brenner/PhotoEdit; 33 (tcl): Steven Peters/Tony Stone Images; 33 (bl): Terry Sinclair/HBC; 33 (br): Wayne Hoy/The Picture Cube; 34 & 35: Joseph Rupp/Black Star/HBC; 40: Alex MacLean/Landslides

Unit 2:
42-43: Larry Ulrich Photography; 43 (bl): HBC; 44 (tl): Andy Sacks/Tony Stone Images; 44 (tc): Burgess Blevins/FPG; 44 (tr): Pete Saloutos/Stock Market; 44 (bl): World Sat Int'l/Science Source/Photo Researchers; 45 (br): Bob Krist/The Stock Market; 45 (tr): Margo Taussig Pinkerton/Gamma-Liaison International; 45 (tr): Rich Franco/HBC; 45 (tc): Rich Iwasaki/Tony Stone Images; 48 (r): John Elk/Tony Stone Images; 48 (l): Peter Correz/Tony Stone Images; 49 (b): David R. Frazier; 49 (t): Richard Paisley/Stock Boston; 50 (both): Ed Cooper; 50: Michael Groen Photography; 50 (br): Fran Antmann; 51 (t): Craig Aurness/Westlight; 51 (bl): J. Randkler/Allstock; 52 (br): Michael Groen Photography; 52 (bl): David Ball/The Stock Market; 52 (tr): George Hunter/Tony Stone Images; 53 (br): Holt Confer/Grant Heilman; 53 (tl): Stephen Simpson/FPG; 56 (tr): Art Wolfe/Allstock; 56 (cl): ChromoSohn/Stock Boston; 56 (b): Frederick McKinney/FPG; 56 (tl): Keith Wood/Tony Stone Images; 57 (cr): Doug Armand/Tony Stone Images; 57 (br): Farrell Grehan/FPG; 57 (bl): Richard Bradbury/Tony Stone Images; 57 (tr): Suzanne Murphy-Larronde/FPG; 58 (b): Buddy Mays/International Stock; 58 (t): Lawrence Migdale; 59 (both): Lawrence Migdale; 60: HBC; 62-63: FPG; 62-63 (bkgrd): Michael Groen Photography; 64 (tl): Andy Sacks/Tony Stone Images; 64 (tr): Chuck Pefley/Allstock; 65 (br): Jerry White/HBC; 65 (tr): Visual Horizon/FPG; 66 (bl): Michael Groen Photography; 66 (tr): S. Nielsen/DRK Photo; 67 (tr): Superstock; 67 (tl): K. Wise/AG Stock USA; 67 (bl): Richard Hutchings/Picture It; 67 (br): Tom Myers/AG Stock USA; 68: Michael Groen Photography; 69: HBC; 82: Michael Groen Photography; 83 (#1): Jim Steinberg/Photo Researchers; 83 (#2): Grant Heilman/Grant Heilman Photography; 83 (#3): Lance Nelson/The Stock Market; 83 (#4): Superstock; 84 (br): Christi Carter/Grant Heilman Photography; 84-85 (t): Randy Taylor/Gamma-Liaison International; 85 (bl): Charlie Westerman/Gamma-Liaison International; 85 (br): Stephen Simpson/FPG; 86 (r): HBC; 86 (l): Lawrence Migdale; 87 (tr & bl): Lawrence Migdale; 87 (c): Phil Degginger/Bruce Coleman; 88 (tr): Corbis/Bettmann; 88 (bl): Lawrence Migdale; 88 (br): Lawrence Migdale/Tony Stone Images; 89 (r): David Austen/Tony Stone Images; 89 (c): John Shaw/Bruce Coleman; 89 (l): Phil Degginger/Bruce Coleman; 90 (both): Courtesy of Tree Musketeers; 90 (frame): Michael Groen Photography; 91 (both): Courtesy of Tree Musketeers; 95 (#1): John Shaw/Bruce Coleman; 95 (#2): Muriel Orans; 95 (#3): Jose Corillo/PhotoEdit; 95 (#4): Norman Tomalin/Bruce Coleman; 95 (#5): Joy Spurr/Bruce Coleman; 97: Michael Groen Photography;

Unit 3:
98 (bl): Peter Vandermark/Stock Boston; 98-99: Lillian Gee/Picture It; 100 (cr): Superstock; 100 (br): Alan Schein/The Stock Market; 100 (tr): Peter Vandermark/Stock Boston; 100 (bl): Porterfield/Chickering/Photo Researchers; 100 (tl): Rich Franco/HBC; 101 (bl): HBC; 101(tl): Jon Riley/Folio; 101 (tc): Joseph Nettis/Tony Stone Images; 101 (tr): Rich Franco/HBC; 104-105: Lawrence Migdale; 105 (tl): Billy E. Barnes/PhotoEdit; 105 (br): Elena Rooraid/PhotoEdit; 106: Michael Groen Photography; 108 (l): Terry Sinclair/HBC; 108-113: Henry Horenstein; 110-111 (c):Terry Sinclair/HBC; 112-113 (c): Rich Franco/HBC; 113 (t &r): Michael Groen Photography; 114 (tl): Ernest Manewal/Superstock; 114 (r): Marleen Ferguson/PhotoEdit; 114 (tl): Nubar Alexanian/Stock Boston; 115 (t & c): HBC; 115 (b): Richard Hutchings/PhotoEdit; 115 (bkgd): Victoria Bowen/HBC; 116 (b): HBC; 116 (c): Coco McCoy/Rainbow; 116 (t): Elena Roraid/PhotoEdit; 116-117 (bkgd): Victoria Bowen/HBC; 117 (t): Superstock; 117 (c): Henry Horenstein; 117 (b): T. Kitchen/Tom Stack & Associates; 118 (b): Terry Sinclair/HBC; 119 (cr): Michael Groen Photography; 119 (tr): Terry Sinclair/HBC; 120-121: Lillian Gee/Picture It; 122-123: Rich Franco/HBC; 123 (t): Michael Groen Photography; 124: HBC; 124 (b): Rich Franco/HBC; 125: HBC; 126: Michael Groen Photography; 128-129: Mark Robinson/Courtesy of Biz Kids; 134: HBC

Unit 4:
136: NASA; 136 (b): U.S. Dept. of the Interior/National Park Service/Edison Nat'l Historical Park; 138 (bl): ChromoSohn/Sohm/The Stock Market; 138 (br): Paul Damien/Tony Stone Images; 138 (tr): Ted Hooper/Folio; 139 (tl): Art Resource; 139 (tr): Culver Pictures; 139 (bl): Edison Natl Park/Natl Park Serv, US Dept. of Interior; 139 (br): Martin De Leon/Still Life Stock; 142 (tr): Corbis/Bettmann; 144 (both): The Granger Collection; 145 (tr): Jerry Jacka; 145 (tl): Joel Gordon; 145 (br): Mus. of Am. Indian/Michael Groen Photography; 148 (bl): David Houser; 148 (br): Michael Phillip Manheim/International Stock; 149 (br): Claudia Parks/The Stock Market; 149 (cr): Ned Haines/Photo Researchers; 149 (tr): Phyllis Picard/International Stock; 149 (bl): Ted Hooper/Folio; 150 (tr): Colonial Williamsburg; 150 (bl): Lou Jones/The Image Bank; 150 (br): Willie Parker/Colonial Williamsburg; 151 (both): Mary Ann Hemphill/Photo Researchers; 154 (t): Bill Stanton/International Stock; 154 (br & bl): Sal Maimone/Photophile; 155: James Blank/Tony Stone Images; 156 (t): Andrews/Photophile; 156 (br & bl): Glasheen Graphics/Photophile; 157 (t): James Blank/The Stock Market; 157 (r): Matt Lindsay/Photophile; 158-159: San Diego Historical Society Photograph Collection; 160 (l): Michael Groen Photography; 160 (r): Tony Stone Images; 161 (tr): Courtesy

For permission to reprint copyrighted material, grateful acknowledgment is made to the following sources:

Atheneum Books for Young Readers, an imprint of Simon & Schuster Children's Publishing Division: Cover illustration from *The Pilgrims of Plimoth* by Marcia Sewall. Copyright © 1986 by Marcia Sewall.

Bantam Doubleday Dell Books for Young Readers: "General Store" from *Taxis and Toadstools* by Rachel Field. Text copyright 1926 by Rachel Field. Cover illustration from *Mrs. Katz and Tush* by Patricia Polacco. Copyright © 1992 by Patricia Polacco.

Charlesbridge Publishing: Cover illustration by Ralph Masiello from *The Flag We Love* by Pam Muñoz Ryan. Illustration copyright © 1996 by Ralph Masiello.

Children's Book Press: Cover illustration from *Family Pictures/Cuadros de familia* by Carmen Lomas Garza, Spanish version by Rosalma Zubizarreta. Copyright © 1990 by Carmen Lomas Garza.

The Lois Lenski Covey Foundation, Inc.: "Sing a Song of People" from *The Life I Live* by Lois Lenski. Text copyright © 1965 by The Lois Lenski Covey Foundation, Inc.

Delacorte Press: Cover illustration by Caroline Binch from *Billy the Great* by Rosa Guy. Illustration copyright © 1991 by Caroline Binch.

Dutton Children's Books, a division of Penguin Putnam Inc.: Cover illustration by Elisa Kleven from *Isla* by Arthur Dorros. Illustration copyright © 1995 by Elisa Kleven.

Mari Evans: "I Can" from *Singing Black* by Mari Evans. Text copyright © 1976 by Mari Evans. Published by Reed Visuals, 1979.

Greenwillow Books, a division of William Morrow & Company, Inc.: Cover illustration from *Music, Music for Everyone* by Vera B. Williams. Copyright © 1984 by Vera B. Williams.

The Hampton-Brown Company: "Orgullo/Pride" by Alma Flor Ada from *A Chorus of Cultures: Developing Literacy Through Multicultural Poetry* by Alma Flor Ada, Violet J. Harris, and Lee Bennett Hopkins. Text copyright © 1993 by Hampton-Brown Books.

HarperCollins Publishers: Cover illustration from *Radio Man* by Arthur Dorros, Spanish translation by Sandra Marulanda Dorros. Copyright © 1993 by Arthur Dorros; translation copyright © 1993 by Sandra Marulanda Dorros. Cover illustration from *Marge's Diner* by Gail Gibbons. Copyright © 1989 by Gail Gibbons. *Winter Days in the Big Woods* by Laura Ingalls Wilder, illustrated by Renée Graef. Text

adapted from *Little House in the Big Woods*, copyright 1932 by Laura Ingalls Wilder, renewed 1959, by Roger Lea MacBride; illustrations copyright © 1994 by Renée Graef.

Houghton Mifflin Company: Cover illustration from *The Giant Jam Sandwich* by John Vernon Lord, verses by Janet Burroway. Copyright © 1972 by John Vernon Lord.

Alfred A. Knopf, Inc.: *How to Make an Apple Pie and see the world* by Marjorie Priceman. Copyright © 1994 by Marjorie Priceman. Cover illustration by Anita Lobel from *A New Coat for Anna* by Harriet Ziefert. Illustration copyright © 1986 by Anita Lobel.

Lothrop, Lee & Shepard Books, a division of William Morrow & Company, Inc.: Cover illustration from *Market!* by Ted Lewin. Copyright © 1996 by Ted Lewin.

Morrow Junior Books, a division of William Morrow & Company, Inc.: Cover illustration by Catherine Stock from *A Very Important Day* by Maggie Rugg Herold. Illustration copyright © 1995 by Catherine Stock. Cover illustration from *Johnny Appleseed* by Steven Kellogg. Copyright © 1988 by Steven Kellogg.

National Geographic Society: Cover illustration from *Young Abe Lincoln* by Cheryl Harness. Copyright © 1996 by Cheryl Harness.

Orca Book Publishers: Cover illustration by Stephen McCallum from *The New Land: A First Year on the Prairie* by Marilynn Reynolds. Illustration copyright © 1997 by Stephen McCallum.

Orchard Books, New York: Cover illustration by John Ward from *We Keep a Store* by Anne Shelby. Illustration copyright © 1990 by John Ward.

Marian Reiner, on behalf of Aileen Fisher: "Always Wondering" from *Always Wondering* by Aileen Fisher. Text copyright © 1991 by Aileen Fisher.

Scholastic Inc.: Cover illustration from *This Is My House* by Arthur Dorros. Copyright © 1992 by Arthur Dorros.

Simon & Schuster Books for Young Readers, an imprint of Simon & Schuster Children's Publishing Division: Cover illustration from *The Keeping Quilt* by Patricia Polacco. Copyright © 1988 by Patricia Polacco.

Tambourine Books, a division of William Morrow & Company, Inc.: Cover illustration by Kathy Osborn from *The Joke's on George* by Michael O. Tunnell. Illustration copyright © 1993 by Kathy Osborn.

Viking Penguin, a division of Penguin Putnam Inc.: Cover illustration from *Eleanor* by Barbara Cooney. Copyright © 1996 by Barbara Cooney.